Stories from The Secret War

To Steve —
Keep it green!
Terry Burke

Stories from The Secret War

CIA Special Ops in Laos

Terrence M. Burke

La Plata Books
DURANGO, COLORADO

Edited by Julie A. Bergman

All statements of fact, opinion, or analysis expressed are those of the author and do not reflect the official positions or views of the CIA or any other U.S.Government Agency. Nothing in the contents should be construed as asserting or implying U.S. Government authentication of information or Agency endorsement of author's views. This material has been reviewed by the CIA to prevent disclosure of classified information.

ISBN 978-0-9883308-0-1

La Plata Books
361 S. Camino del Rio, Suite 103
Durango, CO 81303

Cataloging-in-Publication Data is on file with the Library of Congress

Cover photographs: Terrence M. Burke, Irene Burke and Ralph Holt.
Cover and book design: Isaac Hernández/IsaacHernandez.com.

Manufactured in the United States of America
First Printing: October 2012

This book is dedicated to those who died during
my years working with them in Laos:

CIA officers Don F, Ed Johnson,
Lou O'Jibway, Mike Duel, and Mike Mahoney.

The many Thai Paru who gave their lives for
their neighbors to the north.

The Air America pilots and crews who died
with valor, flying under often unbelievable conditions.

The Meo soldiers who died, not for country,
but for peace for themselves and family.

Prologue

For two and a half decades, a war was carried out in the northern mountains and southern jungles of Laos. This war ran in spurts from the 1950s through 1975 when the Kingdom of Laos ceased to exist and the Lao People's Democratic Republic came into being.

The early years of the war were dominated by the French Army. As the French left Indo China, their presence in Laos was eventually taken over in the early 1960s by American Special Forces teams and a few CIA paramilitary officers.

In 1962, the Geneva Accords was signed. It was an international agreement that called for all foreign troops to leave the Kingdom of Laos. While the United States honored the agreement by removing the U.S. Special Forces teams, the North Vietnamese Army and their Laotian proxies, the Pathet Lao, did not follow suit, but remained a threatening military force in Laos.

Anticipating this development, the CIA had begun training a Thai Police element named the Parachute Resupply Unit, or Paru. Following the withdrawal of the American military, these Thai units, with two American CIA paramilitary officers, clandestinely entered Northern Laos to begin working with a mountain tribal group, the Hmong (or Meo) led by Colonel Vang Pao, a French Military-trained Meo tribesman. Thus began the "Secret War".

The guerilla operations of the CIA with the Meo in the first half of the Sixties eventually gave way to a larger and larger American presence, including the return of the U.S. Military, as the war escalated dramatically during its final decade.

Since the end of the war in 1975, there have been a number of books written providing historical insight into the "Secret War." I have read most of them, some written by authors with great insight and understanding but, unfortunately, some seemingly written in a Vientiane bar while the author listened to war stories from want-to-be warriors.

What I did not find was the real story of the CIA paramilitary officers who fought the secret war in those mountains alongside their Meo and Thai partners. I played a role in this drama from 1963 to 1965 and believed it important to fill that gap. And thus this book.

I have not attempted to make this a historical tome, but through these stories, to place a face on those who lived, worked and sometimes died in an effort to keep a small landlocked kingdom free. I hope that my description of that remarkable time in history will help to do so.

Chapter 1

The stars were clear and bright in the northern Laotian sky at 5AM on May 21, 1965. The trouble was that I should not have been able to see the stars. The thatched hut I that shared with two of my Thai partners had no window in it. My ears were ringing from the shattering noise that had awoken me. I was looking through what, until moments before, had been the side wall of the hut, when the initial mortar round was followed by a second that blew dirt and debris through the gaping hole. The mortars were joined by the sound of automatic weapons fire ripping through our small area of huts that rested on a slight rise above a northern Laotian village.

I shouted to the two Thais to go out the door on the north side of the hut and head towards the dirt airstrip we had just cut out of the jungle. I had slept, as usual, in my fatigue jacket and trousers with my jungle boots on and laced. I pulled several bandoleers of ammunition over my shoulder, shoved grenades in my jacket pocket, and checked the .38 caliber Smith & Wesson that rested in the shoulder holster I had also worn while sleeping. There is something to be said for being paranoid when you are the lone CIA paramilitary officer behind enemy lines within a few miles of both the Chinese and North Vietnamese borders.

The sound of automatic weapons fire, mortars and grenades was growing in intensity by the second. Bending on one knee, I drew my knife from its sheath on my belt and slashed at the plastic overlay on the map board on which I had marked both enemy and friendly positions. I did not want that map to fall into enemy hands.

Two North Vietnamese soldiers, eerily backlit by the first light of dawn that began to brighten the sky, lunged into the doorway. Not seeing me, they began to spray fire from their automatic rifles in an arc starting to their right and turning left towards where I knelt a few feet away.

Chapter 2

The toll of World War II in the early 1940's was marked by "Sons in Service" flags hung in the windows of those mothers who had a son in the active military, indicated by a blue star sewn into the white field of the flag, or who had lost a son, shown by a gold star. I remember seeing some houses along the residential streets of my native Minneapolis, whose "Gold Star Mother's" flags displayed two or three gold stars for one household. I was very young, but I knew there was a war going on. I wanted to be a grownup quickly so that I, too, could go to war.

Even as I grew older though, my timing was still not good enough. I was too young for the fight in Korea, but with my parent's permission, I joined the Marine Corps Air Wing Reserve at the age of sixteen while just a junior in high school. I attended training regularly and a summer three week reserve deployment at El Toro Naval Air Station in Southern California between my junior and senior years of high school.

Following that summer training two things became apparent. First of all, based on my three weeks in California, I learned that not everyone froze a good share of the year as I had in Minnesota, and I had no intention of doing that any longer. Secondly, I had little or no mechanical ability and no one in their right mind would want to fly a plane that I had repaired. Fortunately, the Marine Corps agreed with that assessment and honored my request to transfer to the infantry side of the Corps.

My second summer training after graduation from high school was back in California, but this time at Camp Pendleton and infantry training. I had volunteered for active duty, but I was able to set a reporting date for boot camp at San Diego after the summer training . The reserve experience served me well throughout boot camp. While that 12 weeks was no picnic, at least I knew the basics. Infantry training followed boot camp and then assignment to the 5th Marine Regiment, 1st Marine Division at Camp Pendleton. I became a "Bar Man", carrying the Browning Automatic Rifle with magazines in a pouch belt that really weighed you down.

At the age of nineteen I had completed my two-year active reserve obligation and was eligible to go home and become a member of the part-time reserve. Having yet to see any combat action and not being old enough to buy a beer in most places (like you could on base), and not anxious to return to Minnesota, I volunteered for another three years of active duty. Not long thereafter, I answered a solicitation to be considered for the Marine Embassy Security Guard School at Henderson Hall in Washington D.C. Having passed the screening process, I headed for Washington. Selection for the school was tough, but getting through it and receiving the prestigious assignment to help guard a U.S. embassy in some far-flung land was the prize.

We started with 110 candidates, all of whom had to be at least the rank of corporal and have a spotless record. The best way to describe the intensity of the training was the fact that, of the 110 starters, only 36 of us graduated from that class. There were lighter moments. I circumvented the dreaded scrub duties, when the rest of the class were on their hands and knees cleaning the barracks, by donning a duty belt, grabbing a clipboard, and carrying out fictitious"inspections" of all the fire extinguishers in the building.

One of my goals was to graduate among the top three in the class. The reward was that you could specify three duty posts and be assured you would get one of them. I had that opportunity and chose Moscow, Brussels, and Madrid. To my surprise I was assigned to Rome. When I (humbly) asked 1st Sergeant Radner what had happened to my choices, he advised that he had served in Rome and that it was the best embassy post in the Corps. He had decided that Rome would be more suitable for me and the Corps, and he made the decision for me. I am forever grateful to him.

During my two years in Rome, from 1957 to 1959, I met and married my wife, Irene, who worked as the secretary to the Air Force Defense Attache. It was also where I met and became friends with a number of CIA officers. They began to plant the seed and to encourage me to consider the Agency for a career.

They also emphasized the need to obtain a college education before doing so.

Towards the end of my tour, I was advised that the Corps had screwed up my reenlistment. My choice was to take immediate discharge or reenlist as a "regular" versus a "reserve". The latter meant that at the end of my Rome tour I would be assigned to Camp Lejeune, North Carolina for three years. I chose the immediate discharge, married Irene and we traveled to Washington D.C. for my discharge. Wanting to get college under my belt in order to qualify for the CIA, and obviously having forgotten how cold it was, we headed for Minnesota and St. Thomas College.

During my year at St. Thomas, I answered a CIA ad for employees. The interviewer said that the only positions they had at the Agency for non-college graduates were as communications technicians. I abandoned the idea since I had no experience in communications, but I did want to get back into the international field, so I applied for and was accepted at Georgetown University's School of Foreign Service. With Irene and our three-week old son, Michael, I took off in a white Oldsmobile convertible, pulling everything we owned in a U-Haul trailer, and headed for the East Coast.

Before leaving, I had contacted the former Rome Embassy security chief who was now posted at the State Department in Washington DC. He assured me that I would have a job upon my arrival. After dropping Irene and Michael at Irene's parents in Rhode Island, I arrived in Falls Church, Virginia towing the

U-Haul trailer with all of our possessions. A family friend, the pastor of a Catholic church there, had offered us a residence behind the parish building, in a house which the Church had bought for the future arrival of some Belgium nuns. Our rent would be covered in exchange for mowing the lawns of the church and Irene doing secretarial work for the pastor.

My next stop was a phone booth at Bailey's Crossroads where I telephoned my friend at the State Department. Great anticipation quickly faded to great dismay when I was informed that my friend had suddenly died of a heart attack the week before and that no one else knew of me or any job opportunity. Fairly staggered by this turn of events, I returned to the house and started unpacking the trailer. A gentleman who lived in the house next door soon joined me. I didn't realize it until later, but in the course of helping me carry boxes into the house, he did an excellent job of debriefing me regarding my background. He was particularly interested in who I knew in Rome. I mentioned several Agency friends, maintaining their cover positions in describing them. He also learned of my sudden jobless predicament.

The next evening my new neighbor knocked on the door and gave me a card with the address 1016 16th Street, Washington D.C. written on it. He told me that they would be expecting me and to use his name as reference. He was the director of personnel security for the Central Intelligence Agency and 1016 16th Street was the Agency's processing center for new employees who were awaiting their security clearances. Interestingly, it shared a common wall with an exclusive club whose beautiful hostesses welcomed D.C.'s male elite.

The next weeks were a blur between filling out a million forms, a polygraph examination and all that was required to process my background investigation. The fact that I'd had a Top Secret security clearance from working at the embassy in Rome sped up the process. I was told that I would await the final security clearance by working on a project for the Agency's medical staff. This was especially welcome as it meant moving to the Agency's compound on 23rd Street, across from the State Department (now the site of the E Street Freeway) and working directly with Agency staff.

The assignment was to assist an administer and score written psychological tests that new employees above the clerical level were required to take. As I worked, I overheard comments from medical staff members who were engaged in LSD experiments on unwitting souls. Thus began my education in the clandestine world.

Probably the most significant event of my short tour as an Agency psychological evaluator was the opportunity one day to look into a large, very secret room manned by white-coated technicians. A series of large metal cabinets topped with tall vacuum tubes appeared to be linked by electrical cables. They completely filled a huge two-story room. The only explanation I heard was that it was called "a computer." In 1960, this was a term totally foreign to me. In later years I found it of interest that the CIA had somehow been involved with the development of what is now such a major factor of everyday life throughout most of the world.

Finally my security clearance was granted and I was assigned to the CIA's Office of Physical Security at a salary of $4,040 a year, which was a lot of money to me then. The downside was that my first training by the CIA was learning how to change the combinations of security safes and to replace their broken parts. Those two and four drawer monsters filled the old operational buildings of the CIA that lined one side of the reflecting pool between the Lincoln Memorial and the Capital Building. The only upside was receiving notes from young lady clerks and secretaries that they were suffering from "sticky drawers" and would we please respond so they could more easily close their drawers.

Agency regulations required that safe combinations be changed periodically. Coming up with new three unit combinations for thousands of safes became a real challenge for the handful of us technicians. I fell back on using the same numbers in different sequence for the large doors that separated entire wings of the World War II era buildings. Behind those doors lay the offices staffed by people who handled the Agency's most classified projects. One of the projects was known as "Operation Wave," the Bay of Pigs, or Cuban invasion project. Every morning, scores of admirals, generals and lesser staff entered the building and went through the seven-foot bank vault door into their offices beyond. That is, until one morning when the keeper of the massive vault door failed to arrive to open it. I happened to be walking into the building and saw a large crowd of war planners, some with several stars, eagles and other such rank insignia jiggling on agitated shoulders. I recognized a friend among the throng. He explained the dilemma and asked if I was a safe expert from Security. Not wishing to admit any shortcomings in this area, I readily acknowledged that I was an expert. I was steered to the head of the pack and, facing the vault door, challenged to overcome the locking mechanism in front of an impressive and impatient audience.

I had changed the combination on the vault door not many months before, but the challenge was to remember in which order I had used my favorite numbers, 22-66-44. I requested silence, removed my suit jacket, bent to one knee, and with my ear to the dial, began turning the tumblers. That was how I had seen it done in the movies, but having only three series of numbers to work with definitely placed the odds on my side. After a couple of false passes, and hearing a rising murmur of dissension, I dialed the most likely series, rose, turned the handle and opened the door. I was almost trampled by the ungrateful crowd as they rushed to their offices to complete their plan for a disaster.

With the considerable assistance of my superiors, I was juggling my work schedule with classes at Georgetown. I was offered the opportunity to shift to the Night Security Office, working four to midnight, so that I could take classes in the daytime. Security duties, once the buildings had closed down, were limited to walking down the buckled wooden floored hallways once an hour, making as much noise as possible to waken the slumbering General Services Administration guards before you arrived at their post. This eliminated the necessity of catching them sleeping and having to write them up. The rest of the time was spent either studying or scanning the incoming messages for the Office of Security in case a senior office had to be notified of a significant event.

One of those moments occurred when a CIA station chief in an Asian country sent an "immediate action" cable reporting the arrest of a CIA Office of Security polygraph operator by the local Special Branch police unit. The CIA station had recruited a Special Branch officer and had requested that he have a polygraph to confirm his sincerity. The officer had either reported the station's approach to him or the police had uncovered it. The Special Branch waited until the polygraph examination was being conducted in the CIA security man's hotel room, then kicked in the door and arrested the American officer. The American was held without publicity for some time until no less than Attorney General Robert Kennedy reached an accord with the leader of the country for his release. The compromise that was reached included a promise that the US Government would never again run a unilateral operation in that country. This agreement would have impact decades later, when at the Drug Enforcement Agency, we assigned a DEA agent to that country.

As an Agency security officer, I underwent periodic firearms training in the basement range of the Treasury Building. I never expected to welcome the authority to carry a weapon until late into my shift on a summer night when a distraught female Agency employee called to report she had been sexually assaulted by an intruder in her Georgetown apartment. I quickly contacted the DC Police dispatch and then woke my superior at his home. He instructed me to go to the woman's apartment and provide assistance.

I raced through the quiet streets of Washington to the apartment. To my surprise, I had beaten the police there. The intruder had entered the third floor apartment through a window adjacent to a fire escape. Our employee was badly frightened but quite calm, and she told me that the man had gone out through the same window and gone up the ladder towards the roof.

On the chance that the assailant might have trapped himself there, I went out the window and climbed the fire escape to the roof. From there I could see where he could have crossed from that roof to the next several buildings. There was no sign of him, but I looked down to the street and saw the arrival of the DC Police. Realizing that if they observed a male on the roof with a pistol in hand, they would probably start shooting before asking for ID. I beat a hasty retreat back down the ladder and into the apartment.

As events unfolded throughout the evening, I saw the lengths to which the Agency went to protect and assist their employees.

I was joined at the apartment by other Agency personnel who arranged for medical assistance and stayed with our employee both at the hospital and when she returned home. The Agency later helped her in finding another apartment. The Agency had also arranged with the police that there would be no press report of the incident.

Chapter 3

The failed Bay of Pigs invasion changed many things at the CIA. Suddenly the Agency was thrust into the headlines. Threats were being received against the Director, Allen Dulles. Protests were scheduled at the C Street CIA complex. On a chilly and rainy Saturday morning, another young security officer and I were assigned to coordinate crowd control with the DC Police and to keep security officials inside abreast of the situation by radio.

While waiting in the rain for the arrival of the convoy of buses that was bringing protestors from as far away as New York City, a large puddle of water about six inches deep and 20'x 30' formed in the parking area to one side of the closed front gates. My partner and I gathered the police officers and laid out our plan. As the convoy of buses came down the street in the rain, the police directed the first bus to pull up adjacent to the large puddle. Other police directed the following drivers to keep their doors closed. The first bus driver was then instructed to open his door and discharge his passengers, who had no choice but to wade across the water. Then the first bus was ordered to pull down the street and the second and following buses, one at a time, pulled forward and unloaded their passengers into the puddle.

The protest had been scheduled to last a number of hours. Under DC law the protestors had to keep moving, which they did, parading in long lines in front of the gates, up the street and then back again. Soon however, the chants against the Agency changed to complaints of cold, wet and sore feet from walking in soggy shoes and socks. Organization quickly broke down as more and more protesters returned to the warmth of the buses. Within an hour the demonstration was over and hundreds of protestors were on their way back home. While our superiors obviously could not outwardly condone the action we had taken, there were more than a few pats on the back when we returned inside the gates.

Following this incident, I was asked to help supplement Director Dulles's personal security staff. It sounded like a great assignment. The reality sunk in after about the third night spent in the cramped, damp basement of the Dulles residence where Mrs. Dulles had declared we should be. I suddenly realized why the regular security staff had welcomed my assistance.

What became more interesting was my assignment to accompany the Director when he testified on Capital Hill. The intensity of the aftershock of The Bay of Pigs was tremendous. Director Dulles was summoned before several committees, the most notable being Senator William Fulbright's Senate Foreign Relations Committee. Unfortunately, the Director's idea of the role of the agents assigned to his protection was vastly different from that of the Office of Security. As he swept into the Senate hearing room, Director Dulles would shrug his raincoat from his shoulders and release the attache case from his hand. His expectation was that the security agent behind him had best catch both articles before they hit the floor. I had never been that agile, but I did meet the challenge in those instances. Heaven forbid I might have had to attempt to protect him at the same time.

For a 22 year old, however, these were heady moments. I did not dare discuss the invasion of Cuba operation with my wife or friends. After several closed congressional hearings it became impossible to separate what I had heard in a secret hearing and what I had read in the Washington Post. Therefore, I learned to say nothing; a tough task for a lad who never minded hearing himself talk.

Just as the Cuba invasion issue seemed to calm down, along came the issue of the number of nuclear missiles the Russians had aimed at the United States. Once again, Director Dulles headed back to the Capital with his Deputy Director for Intelligence and his Chief Counsel. The venue was the House Appropriations Committee whose elderly chairman made an opening statement and then fell into a deep slumber. His Deputy Chairman, a Congressman from Texas, ran the rest of the day's proceedings.

The entire morning was devoted to the prepared statement of Director Dulles. It had been established that each committee member would have the opportunity to ask three questions of the Director in the afternoon session. During the testimony I could see the dozen or so members exchanging heated comments and notes with their aides as it became clear that not all of them agreed with the Director's testimony.

Just before the recess for lunch, the Chairman awoke from his slumber and was quietly briefed by his Deputy Chairman. The Chairman then announced that, due to the sensitivity of the testimony, all of his Committee members would leave their notes in the hearing room during the break. The CIA Chief Counsel then advised me that it was their wish that I remain behind so that they could safely leave their briefing books and charts.

In seconds, all had disappeared leaving myself and one Congressional staffer behind. This gentleman stood looking at the closed door. "They are going to crucify Dulles this afternoon", he advised me. "Why so?" I asked in all innocence. He told me that just two days earlier, the Chairman of the Joint Chiefs of Staff had given a briefing on Russian ballistic missile strength that totally contradicted what Dulles had said that morning. The Deputy Chairman had called the Pentagon to bring their charts up immediately so they could flatten Dulles. "They are on their way now," the Congressional staffer said. While I absorbed this, he bemoaned the fact that he had personal errands to run, had not had breakfast and really needed the time before the hearing resumed to resolve these issues. I assured him that I would be happy to cover for him and that I would keep everything safe until his return.

Locking the door behind him, I turned and pondered how to take advantage of the situation. I began moving across the elevated platform where each Congressional committee member sat. Looking at each member's portion of the lengthy desk, I realized that most of them had written out, or been provided by their staff, the three allotted questions they would have the opportunity to ask of Director Dulles. I quickly began noting the congressman's name and recording his questions. They ranged from the inane to some very penetrating questions. One of those who had very good questions was the Congressman from Michigan named Gerald Ford.

No sooner had I completed recording the questions than there was a loud knocking on the committee room door. Upon opening it I was confronted by an Army officer and several enlisted men carrying large leather briefing chart bags. Assuming the role of Congressional host and security director, I instructed them where to place the bags. We then stood and looked at each other. Being good military men, they almost immediately began complaining that they had been sent on their mission without the benefit of their noon meal. Being the good host, I responded by providing them with directions to the Congressional cafeteria complete with assurances that their charts would be maintained in a most secure environment.

Once the door was locked again, I went to work. The chart cases were opened and notes of the facts they presented were taken. The next step was a call to the Office of Chief Counsel. After penetrating several layers of that bureaucracy I was finally speaking to the Chief Counsel. Using double-talk I advised that it was in the best interest of the Agency that he and/or the Deputy Director return to the hearing room in advance of the afternoon's session. "This better be good," said the GS 18 to the GS 4.

About thirty minutes before the session was to resume, the Chief Counsel arrived. I provided him with the list of questions for each Committee member and my summary of the figures from the Joint Chief of Staff's charts (which were again securely back in their cases guarded by the now well-fed soldiers). He grunted.

A short time later, the Deputy Director joined the General Counsel and the two quietly read my notes. Once or twice, the Deputy looked down the table at me, totally expressionless. Well, I thought, I can always go back to bartending. The two then began to go through their briefing books, scribbling comments next to my notes. Director Dulles arrived a few minutes before the session was to start. He stood in quiet conference with his Deputy and the General Counsel, pouring over the notes. When finished, the Director looked down the end of the room staring over his glasses directly at me. His expression told me nothing. I immediately began to try to remember the recipes for favorite bar drinks.

The afternoon session belonged to Director Dulles. As each congressman asked his questions, Director Dulles glanced briefly at his notes, looked to the ceiling as he puffed his pipe, then provided the smoothest answers ever heard in a committee hearing room. His counters to the facts provided on the military charts were no less eloquent. At the end of the session all of the committee members took turns trying to outdo each other in complimenting Director Dulles on his presentation. I noted that the very pleasant young congressman Gerald Ford was among the most effusive in his praise.

All went quiet for the next few days. I was told that my services on the Director's protective staff were no longer needed. I returned to the Physical Security staff and waited for the other shoe to drop. It was not long in coming. I was suddenly advised that I was to appear before the Director of Security at a certain hour that afternoon. The man was a legend. Tough and hard with the ability to tear your heart out with his bare hands, so went the stories. I thought of all of that as I stood in front of his imposing desk as ordered. Quietly, but with force, he informed me that Director Dulles himself wished to make it totally clear to me that the CIA did not spy on members of the United States Congress nor on their military brethren at the Pentagon. My actions were totally contrary to the CIA's charter.

I stood stunned as Director of Security paused. "But", he finally continued, "The Director asked me to tender his thanks for your assistance." In a state of shock I continued to listen as he advised that they had looked at my short record at the Agency and were pleased. They had also looked at my efforts to raise a family of three and pay my own tuition at Georgetown on that grand sum of $4,040 a year. He was offering me the position of assistant security officer at the Agency's domestic training station where on-base housing would be available at $60 per month and where the Agency had already arranged for my transfer from Georgetown University to a nearby college.

Chapter 4

The training site was quite a change from Washington DC. At that time the fact that the training base was a CIA operation was highly classified. It would not be until a number of years later that the true ownership of the base came known. The Security Chief and the second security officer were both highly experienced officers and great to work with. The housing was a tiny house at the end of the base, but the price was right.

The real fascination was meeting and getting to know the training staff, largely composed of long time Agency case officers who had served in all parts of the globe. Some of them were of considerable renown, such as the famous Soviet Colonel Penkovsky's case officer. It would not take too many drinks in the officer's club to hear his fascinating tales of running one of the top and most productive moles within the Soviet military during the height of the Cold War.

My interest was drawn to the staff of agency trainers who ran the paramilitary training program. These men were expert in guerilla tactics, weapons, parachuting, demolitions use, raids and ambushes. Several had served the Agency in Tibet, Korea,

Africa and other locations. Their chief had dropped into Yugoslavia in World War II to fight with Tito and his guerrillas against the Germans. They taught tactics and skills to both CIA case officers and certain foreign assets who were brought into the base in the middle of the night, landing at the base airstrip under blacked out conditions. One objective was to keep them from learning where they had been trained throughout the duration of their training.

One of my less glamorous jobs was to scour the forests where they would be living and training for any item that would identify the location of the base. This included cigarette packs with Virginia tax stamps and Coca Cola bottles with "Norfolk, Virginia" on the bottom. I also picked up their meals three times a day at the mess hall, again ensuring that bread packaging, etc did not reveal our location. The contact I had with the mess hall staff was especially rewarding. I soon became fast friends with the mostly African-American cooks and servers who always made sure there was enough food to keep me full as well. Those grits tasted great at 5:00AM on a cold and damp winter morning.

It was impossible for me to accept that in the early 1960's, a US Government facility, no matter under whose auspices it was run, had signs in the staff area at the mess hall and motor pool designating "colored" and "white" toilets and water fountains. I delighted in driving the local white guys at the base motor pool crazy by consistently using the "colored" toilet and water fountain. After a while they apparently wrote me off as a "dumb Yankee," although I'm sure some held stronger opinions.

Eventually, I was asked by the paramilitary (PM) staff if I would serve as an aggressor during the training exercises they held for their students. In one of the secure areas of the base a long fence had been built complete with guard towers. The fence replicated the various types of fences that ringed the Soviet Union and their satellite countries. Many a night I stood in one of the towers or walked as a sentry, eager to spoil the efforts of the students to make it safely through. Other assignments included ambushing student patrols and accompanying students in nighttime infiltration of the base using small rubber craft driven by silenced outboard motors. In addition to all the fun I was having, I was receiving very welcome overtime pay.

All of this activity was taking a toll on my college studies. Evening classes in economics just didn't hold the same excitement as helping foreign trainees who were honing the skills they would need to infiltrate back into their countries and conduct sabotage operations against the repressive governments there. The other problem was that I was no longer satisfied with just the training end of paramilitary operations. I wanted to be in on the action. Growing up during World War II and after, I became a vociferous reader of all accounts of irregular warfare such as the Chindit Bandits in Burma, the partisan forces in Eastern Europe and the underground resistance fighters in a number of European countries. I eventually built a considerable collection of books on the escapes of allied prisoners from prisoner of war camps.

My chance came when a senior official from CIA Headquarters who had been visiting the base frequently was named head of the Agency's new Special Operations Division (SOD). This division was to bring together the clandestine air and ground operations of the Agency to face the challenges coming from Southeast Asia, particularly Vietnam and Laos. Since the Korean War, the PM operations of the Agency had languished as the "classic" clandestine arts operators struggled with what do with the PM "knuckle draggers" left over from the Korean era. Suddenly, however, the importance of PM operators again emerged.

With the intercession of the new head of SOD, I was transferred from the Support Division of the Agency and the Office of Security, to the SOD. I also dropped my classes. I joined a new class of nine paramilitary trainees for what was to be six months of seven days a week training that often went long into or through the night. Seven of the trainees were new graduates of the Agency's Junior Officer Trainee (JOT) Program. Most had come to the JOT program from college, with some having already earned graduate degrees. They had just completed two years of basic training in the clandestine arts and a few of the best from each JOT class would now continue their training in the paramilitary program. The remaining trainee and I were the only "internal" Agency employees in the class.

The weeks raced by as we studied weapons, land navigation, ambush and raid tactics, rappelling, and physical fitness. There were periodic tests of our new skills. The instructor would field strip three different types of weapons and dump the parts in a duffle bag. Blindfolded, you had to reassemble the three weapons in less than five minutes. Night after night we were in the field practicing our techniques. Now it was my turn to curse the "aggressor" forces. For six weeks we went to another site where, in detail, we learned the art of demolitions. We were taught how to blow up everything from houses to bridges, to make our own booby traps and to blow a train from its tracks. I developed a very decent proficiency in this area, which was later to come into good use.

Then we went back to the base for parachute training. The staff followed the basic military course taught at Fort Benning, Georgia. Jumping out of towers, off platforms, and doing endless parachute landing falls (PLFs) became a daily grind. Finally there was the thrill of three daytime jumps out of a C46, one night jump from the same aircraft, and then a jump from a small single engine aircraft.

Then there was more weapons training, emergency medical training, and guerrilla tactics. Close to the end of the course we went to the Army's Jungle Warfare Training Center (JWTC) in Panama for their three-week course. The nine of us were quite a sight. They had allowed us to bring our own jungle boots and hats but insisted we leave our well-worn fatigues behind. They issued us baggy new fatigues, still covered with little white stickers, whose purpose we never figured out.

When we showed up in the first formation, we drew many stares and snickers from the Army Special Forces, Navy Seals, and Marine Recon types who made up the bulk of our fellow trainees. They were all resplendent in starched fatigues with badges, berets and other signs of military prowess.

The first exercise was intended to humble these men who represented elite units in their services. We were trucked into the jungle and dropped, team-by-team, at certain spots along the road. We were given compass coordinates to a distant location. If you located the first marker you would find coordinates to a second destination. A third, fourth and fifth destination then followed, each bearing off the previous one. The exercise was conducted at night under combat light conditions. It was an instant introduction to the black palm tree whose barbed spikes penetrated the toughest leather glove to imbed in your hand like a fishing hook. We met new varieties of insects, most of which were intent on taking pints of your blood with each bite. We found mounds of stinging ants to walk through in the dark and heard the ominous splash of large snakes in the streams we were constantly crossing. Welcome to Panama!

The good news was that six months of constant navigation training paid off. The nine of us, in two separate teams, successfully completed the course at the final destination at the base area, took a quick shower and were working on our second beer at the Officer's Club well before the first muddy military participants showed up. Because they had encountered us at various points in the course, they knew we were out there with them. Questions of "Who are you guys really?" began that night and followed us through the rest of the course.

As I climbed the largest tree I had ever imagined existed, I marveled how training could bring an individual to put a rope loop around his body and then step off a platform some 100 feet off the ground. I roared down the main rope on a pulley with the faith that the knotted rope at the far side of the Chagras River would stop me before the massive tree on the far bank would. It worked. The objective was to demonstrate how a large number of personnel could be moved across a major obstacle (the swift moving Chagras River) in as short period of time using minimal equipment. While flying across that river at an estimated speed of 35 mph I had my doubts, but when I hit the knot at the far end and did a 360-degree flip in the air and came to an abrupt stop, I had to agree it was possible.

The jungle course also taught me that, while training for specific threats is important, it is also wise to accept that general theories can also be applicable. A young Special Forces Captain had spent several hours with the entire class teaching about the dangerous snakes of Panama. We watched while a huge Anaconda devoured two live chickens; their still wriggling bodies misshaping the snake's form. We observed the Vine snake hit a target with its venom, leaving it withering, then dead in minutes.

However, the most impressive and lasting portion of the Captain's presentation was his description of how the Bushmaster snake would pursue and kill a human victim. At length, the Captain pointed out the shape and coloring characteristics of the Bushmaster, intent on insuring we would never fail to quickly identify this dangerous snake if we encountered it in the jungle.

A couple of days later, my team happened to draw this same Captain as our advisor on a field exercise. The five of us moved slowly down the sloping jungle trail, alert for the ambush we were sure had been set up in anticipation of our route. Suddenly, five pairs of eyes focused to our left. Down a tree, just off the trail, pirouetting around the trunk, was a bicep-thick snake obviously intent on being the ambush party we never imagined. "Run!" was probably the most quickly executed command that young Special Forces captain ever gave. Five bodies hurtled down the path in total panic. We sprinted for hundreds of yards in the hot sticky morning heat. As our energy began to wane and panic subside, we finally came to a stop, lungs heaving and burning. One of the team caught his breath. "Was that a Bushmaster, Captain?" he asked. "Dammed if I know," came the expert reply, "Out here they all look like Bushmasters to me!"

One of the high points of the training was the "Individual Reaction Course". The basic assignment was simple. Each trainee was told that his unit was behind enemy lines. The mission was to act as a courier, carrying a verbal message through the enemy to friendly forces at a given point on the map several miles away.

You were instructed to note and report any enemy information you developed en route. Armed with an M1 rifle, several clips of blank ammo, and a few dummy grenades, you set off on the timed course. Over the years the school had developed a number of well-thought-out challenges for this route. The trail was replete with booby traps, including camouflaged pits, and dummies in enemy uniform that suddenly swung from behind trees. Each "challenge point," was secretly observed by an instructor, who graded you on your reaction.

While speed was important, patience and caution were also rewarded. Pausing to scan a particularly open and exposed section of jungle, I sensed the need to take extra time before crossing the clearing. I remained motionless, peering from a concealed position. As I slowly scanned the area, I saw a slight movement from behind a downed tree ahead and to my right. I focused on it, but saw nothing more. Maybe it had been a bird or lizard. As I prepared to rise and move forward, I took one last look at the area and realized I was looking at camouflage netting. I stared harder and located the brush-wrapped barrel of a machine gun poking through the netting, pointed up the trail in the direction they had expected the next trainee to come. At that point I was just off the trail.

I was never much of a pitcher, but this time my aim was straight and my dummy grenade hit the netting and, judging from the pained and angry yell from the "enemy" soldier behind the gun, some part of his anatomy. I didn't wait to exchange pleasantries, but shouted my trainee number as I sprinted past the machine gun emplacement and continued down the trail, wondering what kind of score the unhappy instructor would give me for that station.

Additional challenges of the course included coming across the body of an "enemy " soldier face down just off the trail. Quickly placing a loop of parachute cord around his wrist, I retreated behind a tree and, pulling on the cord, rolled him over onto his back. The booby trap hand grenade that was hidden under his body popped and emitted a small puff of smoke. A fast search of the body yielded a map showing enemy positions. I stuffed this in my shirt pocket, noted his unit insignia, and hurried towards the friendly position. There I reported the assigned message, my observations of enemy locations, and the intelligence I had obtained from the booby-trapped body.

Several days later the scores of the entire class were posted. All of the CIA team was in the top percentage of the class. I had obtained the highest score in the class. My good friend, Don, was just a few points behind me. The final phase of the three-week course was an escape from a mock prisoner of war camp. Late one afternoon the entire class was taken many miles from the base to a barbed wire compound in the jungle. We were told that we had 36 hours to make it back to the base. Each of us had a map, compass, knife, first aid kit, and two canteens on our web belt. Other than water purification tablets, that was it. You could go it alone, in pairs, or as a team. There would be aggressor forces along the way seeking to capture us. Each person carried three tags, each bearing his student number. If you were captured, you gave up one of your tags to the aggressor and continued on your way to the base. The loss of each tag deducted points from your overall score. The loss of all three tags meant you were "dead" as far as scoring went.

Our CIA team decided to break into two groups, one of five and the other of four. I drew a place on the four-man team. We rightfully guessed that there would be an aggressor line fairly close to the prisoner camp. As we expected, most of the trainees broke from the camp on signal, heading eastward in the direction of the base. We headed south instead, turning east only when we heard the chatter of machine guns that announced that many of the trainees had lost their first tag within a short distance of the camp. During the rest of that night and into the next day, we utilized a strategy that I had developed from my reading of World War II escape books. We got within hearing range of a team that was in front of us, and then we shadowed them from behind and to one side. While they moved cleanly, we moved with them. When they ran into an aggressor team or were ambushed, we slid off further on their flank and passed them and the aggressor team, without either becoming aware of our presence. As we moved on, we were alert for another team that we could also us as a decoy in the same manner.

Late that next afternoon we reached the Chagras River. As we had learned in our earlier river crossing by rope, the breadth of the river and the current made swimming across a real challenge. We studied the map for a location to enter the water where the current would take us to the narrowest point on the river on the track we had chosen to reach the base. This meant moving upriver along the bank some distance. We secured our gear on our bodies and emptied our canteens that were in their holders attached to the web belt we all wore. The canteens became our "life jackets", helping us to keep afloat.

My three team members chose to remove their boots and, tying the laces together, hung them around their necks. For whatever reason, I decided to keep mine on. We went into the water after carefully searching the banks and river for aggressors. It took about thirty minutes to approach the far shore, all the while watching for the approach of aggressors by boat. We were just short of the shore when we heard the roar of a motor and saw a boat bearing down on us. As it was about to reach us, I could feel sand under my flailing feet. I was up and out of the water and running into the jungle while my bootless comrades were overtaken by the aggressors. The latter shouted at me to stop, but I kept running. I was only a night and day away from the camp and I was determined not to be "captured".

Continuing the course to the base camp and final destination by myself was not a welcome choice, but there was no other. Once inland away from the river and sure the aggressors had not followed me, I stopped to carefully study the map. I discovered that there was an above ground two-foot pipeline that cut through the jungle within about a mile of my present position. The line followed a fairly straight track towards the base camp, veering off course only in the last couple of miles. If I could use the pipeline as a guide, I could save a lot of time in navigating, as long as I could determine where to leave the pipeline and head directly to the camp.

Within an hour I had located the pipeline. At first I tried to parallel it, figuring that the aggressors might be covering it. Then when I realized how overgrown it was, it was pretty clear that there had not been anyone in the area for a long time. I climbed on top of it and, although there were vines, branches and the like over the pipe, I made fairly good time along the top. At one point it became so entangled that I dropped off and resumed paralleling it. I found a stream with about a five-foot bank running along side of the pipe. The stream was fairly clear of brush and shallow, so my rapid progress continued, until I saw a snake drop over the edge of the bank just ahead and to my right, move down into and across the stream. When its head cleared the top of the five-foot bank to my left and its body was still coming over the right bank, I realized I was seeing an Anaconda in its natural habitat. At that point I decided that the entangled pipeline was definitely the better choice. That night I slept with my back against the pipe. The vision of that monster snake woke me more than once.

The next day I reached a point where it was fairly clear that the pipeline swung away from the base, so I struck out on a direct heading for the base through the jungle. During my approach to the base I calculated the time since we had initiated our escape. I figured that the aggressor forces, from experience, knew how long it would take the escapees to reach the base and would have withdrawn their lines to the base perimeter. A reconnaissance of the perimeter confirmed this. Every so often the sound of blanks being fired confirmed their location and the fact that some weary escapees had stumbled on their lines.

The thought of a cleansing shower and a good meal almost caused me just to make a dash for it, but having made it this far unscathed, pride kicked in and I decided I had to figure out a way. I had gotten quite close to the main gate and realized there were no aggressors there, only the usual gate guards sweating out a standard eight hours of waving folks through the gate. A few hundred yards down from the gate I discovered a base garbage truck stopped at refreshment stand while the Panamanian driver and his helper had a coke or the local equivalent. As they pulled out from the stand I merely swung on to the back step of the truck, out of their sight, and rode through the gate with them.

I was reveling in successfully turning in all of my tags and joining the small group of trainees who had enjoyed the same success, when in the door walked the seven member Navy SEAL Team part of our training contingent. They wore the same fatigues we all had when we made our escape, except theirs' were clean and pressed, they were clean and shaved and their only sign of strain were obvious hangovers. It turns out that from previous Seals who had attended the course, they had learned the general location of the "prison camp." On the weekend prior to the exercise they had gone to Colon where they hired a local with a closed van. When the escape took place, they headed in the opposite direction of the base and met the van on a nearby road. While we were swimming the Chagras and getting the hell scared out of us by Anacondas, they were enjoying the fleshpots of Colon. Their driver drove them back to the base gate where the guards, seeing their neat uniforms, waved them in. So much for "jungle savvy."

Chapter 5

As a final graduation exercise from the Paramilitary Course, we went off to a forested base in east-central Virginia. The scenario was that an enemy force had established a missile site on the base. We had five days to conduct reconnaissance, locate the site and blow it up. We were to live off the land with minimal rations, report all military activity, and avoid discovery by the aggressor forces and everyone else on the base as all had been warned of our presence and ordered to report any sightings. The terrain was somewhat hilly and well forested.

Living off the land became a bit easier when we learned that base work parties would go to various areas of the base daily to perform general maintenance duties. They would go out by truck and tend to their chores, leaving their insulated containers of warm lunch and cold drinks in the back of the trucks. Needless to say, we gained, rather than lost weight that week.

We eventually located the missile site. The missile must have made someone very proud. They had welded 55-gallon gas drums together into a vertical stack about 25 feet high, and constructed a nose cone and painted it silver. The missile site was ringed with every type of barbed wire imaginable and guards were posted on each corner. At night they lit the area with powerful spotlights. We realized immediately that it would be nearly impossible to get the 50 pounds of real explosives we had been supplied close enough to the missile to destroy it. We did discover, however, that a decent sized stream ran through the site. We backtracked upstream until about a half a mile away, we found where energetic beavers had created a sizeable dam adjacent to a steel bridge that ran across the stream. Although we had to duck for cover frequently due to military truck and jeep traffic on the bridge, we managed to rig a "pole charge" with our entire bundle of explosives secured to a strong pole we cut from the forest. The charge was lowered into the water to a depth of about eight feet where the current held it tight against the center of the beaver dam, just in front of the center of the bridge.

The protocol for the exercise called for us to notify the military when we had set the charges, so their personnel could be withdrawn to safety before we turned the crank and sent their missile skyward in many pieces. That scenario presumed we had successfully infiltrated their site and set the charges in close enough proximity to their missile to cause damage. We, however, were a half a mile away without a clue as to whether our charge would even breach the beaver dam, much less send enough water downstream to have any effect. So why should we have to warn them? In any event, that is the story we agreed on before turning the crank that sent the current to the primacord, which burned underwater to the detonators buried in the explosives.

It was a lovely, if not uncxpected, waterspout that erupted from the depths of the stream. Water surged upward and outward breaching the center of the thick dam and cleaving a 20-foot gap through which the stream roared. Despite the classes we had on the subject, we were amazed to see the steel girders of the bridge buckle and tear under the force of the waterspout that rose beneath it.

While anxious to witness the results of our endeavors downstream, the report radioed to us by our team members stationed on a small knoll overlooking the site, caused caution to prevail. We hustled from the area in the opposite direction to meet up with the party that was to extradite us from the base. Apparently, the military at the missile site did not appreciate losing their gear, missile, some vehicles, and communication equipment to the stream that roared through the site, not to mention having to run to keep from being swept away themselves. They became even less enchanted with our success when they had to spend the night in their trucks, not being able to make it back to their quarters past the demolished bridge.

Chapter 6

With graduation at hand and assignments being handed out, we made the transition from trainee to operations officers. Because of the "need to know" principle, we were not always sure what assignment lay ahead for our comrades. Some very strong friendships had been formed, so we tried to keep in touch. My first offer for assignment was to become a demolitions instructor training new paramilitary trainees. While I considered the offer a complement, I was too anxious to get into operations to consider it. Thus I wound up in CIA Headquarters in Langley, Virginia, with onward assignment to the secret paramilitary operation in Laos. The operation was run out of Udorn, Thailand with support from a joint US-Thai location in Nong Khai, Thailand, perched on the Thai side of the bank of the mighty Mekong River.

I was the first married officer assigned to the project. My wife and now two sons (Sean had been born in Williamsburg) would have to reside in Bangkok. Preparing for and executing the move was not made easier by the fact that I was going to Thailand undercover. None-the-less, we flew to Bangkok and checked into the Oriental Hotel as directed. Unfortunately, that hotel did not gain its luxury status for some years later. Within a day or two an officer from the project showed up at the hotel to take me "north." I gave Irene all the money I could spare and promised to return as soon as possible. Her account of dealing with a very foreign city in a hotel with two young boys, knowing no one, is a story in itself. She did so for several weeks, however, much to her credit.

On my return to Bangkok, we learned that colleagues had identified a large house for us. Our effects soon arrived, a couple of servants were hired and I was set to return north again.

My first assignment in the project was to the joint unit in Nong Khai. This turned out to be a large house in the sleepy little Thai border town. Four other Americans were assigned there along with members of the Thai Paru, a special Thai Police paramilitary unit trained and supported by the CIA. The unit received messages from project teams all over Laos, reporting enemy locations and activities, friendly locations, and engagements between the two. The most frequent messages were for rice and ammunition re-supply drops. The mission of the unit was to assess the reports and report enemy moves and project their intentions.

My CIA colleagues turned out to be first class professionals who worked seven days a week, from early morning, long into the night. One was a brilliant Army officer, seconded to the Agency. He had the ability to read through stacks of messages, often written on one-time coded pads from the heart of battle, and come up with an uncanny analysis of what was taking place. He was well supported by one of the few African-American CIA officers at that time. Ed and Captain Bill were the cement that held the Nong Khai operation together. While younger officers like Terry Q. and myself were chomping at the bit to leave the intelligence operation and get into the action in Laos, these two professionals kept the ship on course. Ed had left his wife in suburban Washington D.C. for this assignment. Unfortunately I was not to meet her until over two years later, after Ed perished in a helicopter that crashed in the Mekong River.

Life was not always dull in Nong Khai. We constantly found ways to amuse ourselves or harass our colleagues. Our American administrative officer was unfortunate enough to be struck with hepatitis or yellow jaundice. He was allowed to remain in Nong Khai but had to spend most of the day and night in his room. He was on a strict diet with orders that he could not drink or engage in any type of sexual activity.

After a long day at the unit, we retired to the Happy All Day Bar, a thatched-roof, open-air shack perched precariously on the bank above the river. Singha beer had not yet reached its present day worldwide renown, but the large cold and inexpensive bottles were welcomed in the late evening heat. After enough of these, we would start feeling sorry for our admin officer and his lonely and dull recuperation. On more than one occasion we instructed one of the bar girls, put her in a bicycle taxi (samlor), and sent her off to our house. She went to the patient's locked bedroom door and explained in great detail all of the things she wanted to do to his body as well as what she would like him to do to hers. For unknown reasons he never expressed his thanks for our consideration.

The Happy All Day Bar was also the intended meeting place for a senior Washington, D.C. Headquarters official to debrief Tony Poe, the legendary paramilitary officer stationed at the Lao headquarters of the Project at Long Tieng. An issue had arisen over one of Tony's earlier escapades elsewhere in the world and the officer had flown to Thailand to interview him. Tony was instructed to come to Nong Khai for the meeting, but had resisted for several days until he was threatened with permanent removal from Laos. In the meantime, the senior official was left steaming in Nong Khai, anxious to get out of there. I drew the assignment of picking up Tony at the dirt airstrip just outside of town. Tony tumbled out of the small Helio-Courier as the sun was setting. He was unshaven, dirty, dragged an M-1 rifle behind him and showed obvious signs of having spent the two-hour flight drinking.

Tony refused to be taken to the meeting then, stating he would meet the "Headquarters Hump" the next day. I dropped him at our boss's house and returned to the bar to try to placate the official. The next morning I helped a very hung-over Tony into the Land Rover and took him to the bar. As he walked in and headed for the official who sat at a table, Tony spotted a young girl sleeping in a hammock chair. Tony stopped, lifted her long skirt, peered intently under it, and suddenly and loudly declared, "She's a Vietnamese!" Tony bent down, swooped the girl out of the chair, and proceeded out through the bar door, across the street, and into what passed for the local hotel.

The scene was too much for the official. He stormed from his table, ordering me to take him to the airstrip and to make sure there was a plane there to get him out of this "nuthouse." All the way to the strip he fumed and declared he would have Tony's job. Fortunately, my radio call had caught the pilot and the plane's single propeller was already turning over when we arrived. The official jumped out of the Land Rover, ducked his head and climbed into the rear door of the plane. The plane started to taxi to the end of the strip, then suddenly turned and came back to where I was parked. The rear door opened and the official gestured for me to come to the plane. I ran to the open door, bending over to keep from eating all of the dust being kicked up. Over the roar of the engine the official, with his face contorted by the prop blast and puzzlement, shouted, "How could he tell she was Vietnamese?"

Chapter 7

By the fall of 1963, I was anxious to get out of the Nong Khai and into an operational role. The time there had given me the opportunity to learn what was going on throughout Laos and the enemy locations as well as one could learn from the maps that spread from floor to ceiling. It was obvious that it had also given Bill and Pat, the two Project directors in Udorn, the chance to see if they wanted to keep me around and if I qualified in their eyes to work on my own.

I had passed muster on both issues. The first sign of that was their approval of my request to move Irene and the two boys from Bangkok to Udorn. Udorn was also the base for the Air America operations. A number of the pilots had their American and Asian wives living there and I knew Irene would fit right in. We loaded our household effects, the one Thai maid who had agreed to accompany us, and ourselves in an Air America C46 at the Bangkok Airport. In a few hours, after threading our way through monsoon thunderstorms, we were in Udorn and shortly thereafter in our new house on stilts at the edge of town.

Although still living in Nong Khai, I often made the 30-minute flight back and forth between Udorn and Nong Khai in the shuttle Helio Courier, a single engine short landing and takeoff (STOL) aircraft. One of the pilots delighted in flying literally on the deck, either scaring the workers in the rice fields or playing "chicken" with an oncoming bus on the road. Fortunately, most of the other pilots were content to take a short nap while I got some piloting experience. I brought Irene up to Nong Khai on one of these flights to show her where I had been living and working. Unfortunately I had mentioned these plans to a Nong Khai colleague. As we drove from the airstrip along the dusty street that ran the length of the town, on each corner we encountered one of the young Thai girls from the Happy All Day Club. As we passed, each one called out the same greeting, "Hey Mr. Terry, you very good last night! You number 1!" After the third or fourth girl, Irene turned to me and said, "You're not that good."

The second sign of my acceptance for field work came when I was advised that the two paramilitary officers assigned to the Eastern Thai town of Nakhon Panhom, were going on home leave and I was to fill in for them during their absence. I arrived there to find that the two had worked very hard to establish and direct what was referred to as "Roadwatch Teams" that operated across the Mekong River in the south central "panhandle" of Laos. The purpose of the teams was to establish positions from which they could observe, photograph, and report on North

Vietnamese supply traffic along what later became known as the "Ho Chi Minh Trail." I knew that the officers, Dick and Richard, were under orders not to cross into Laos, but that they were too determined to make sure that the operations were being carried out properly not to make an occasional nighttime trip across the river, at least to the staging camp located several miles into Laos.

During my two months in Nakhon, I made one such crossing myself. I felt very uncomfortable on the trip, not out of fear of capture, but because I had developed considerable distrust for some of the Thai officers, and I had little regard for the "Low Land" Laotians we were forced to work with in that part of the country. Working with this particular team of Thais for paying and directing the Laotians was frustrating. I had struggled to learn a mixture of Thai and Lao while in Nong Khai. While I couldn't really speak further than what might pass in the market, I did understand enough to know that the Thais were not always telling the Laotians what I told them to say. I also knew that what the Laotians were saying was not always what was being relayed to me by the Thais. My greatest concern was that the Lao teams were being outfitted and paid and leaving their camp destined for the Trail, only to stop a safe distance from it and radio in concocted reports. It did appear, however, that on occasion at least some of the teams got close enough to take photos of trucks and elephants carrying supplies towards South Vietnam.

I welcomed the return of Dick and Richard. I briefed them on my activity and my concerns. They apparently had experienced the same qualms, but Dick's fluency in French had allowed him better direct control over the Laos than I had been able to muster. I wished them well and headed back to Udorn for a new assignment. It was not long in coming.

Chapter 8

Long Tieng had been established as the base of operations for the hill tribe Meo (or Humong as they have become known) chieftain, Vang Pao. Vang Pao had risen to the rank of Colonel and then general in the Royal Lao Army. He had been named as Lao Military Region 5 Commander after a retreat of his forces from the Plaine de Jars (PDJ). Much has been written about General Vang Pao and the Meo people he led. With the signing of the Geneva Accords in July 1962, wherein it was agreed that all foreign troops would leave Laos, the U.S. withdrew approximately 600 U.S. Special Forces personnel from Laos which had been supporting the Royal Lao Army and the Meo forces. In their place, the CIA assigned two paramilitary officers to assist General Vang Pao. Guidance to these officers came from the two senior operations officers who worked out of a small facility in Udorn, Thailand.

The original two officers assigned to the project could not have been more different in backgrounds and personalities. Vint was an Ivy League graduate with an excellent command of the French language. He had the ability to transcend his New England establishment background and develop an understanding of the hill tribe people and their leader. During his time at Long Tieng, he worked to guide and cajole Vang Pao towards military, economic, and political objectives.

Tony Poe, the hero of the earlier escapade in Nong Khai, came from a family whose roots had been in Czechoslovakia. His father retired as a Navy Commander after thirty-five years in the service. Tony's time in the Marine Corps in the Pacific during WWII and CIA paramilitary assignments in Korea, Indonesia and Tibet had created a very rough veneer and a desire to create an image for himself as one of the last great warriors. His bravery and exploits under fire proved the image to be well-deserved, but his pursuit of that legend often became self-defeating, especially when alcohol became a predominant factor in his life.

Just as my temporary assignment in Nakhon Panom came to an end, Vint became very ill and had to be med-evacuated to the United States. Bill and Pat, the two chiefs in Udorn, were in a quandary as to who to send to Long Tieng to replace him. Their decision was to send me there to work for Tony Poe. Because of my lack of experience and language ability, it was planned that Bill would visit Long Tieng frequently to meet with Vang Pao. My status in Laos would be such that the assignment had to be approved through the CIA Chief of Station in Vientiane and by the top officials of CIA in Washington, D.C.

I flew from Udorn in a Helio Courier. Crossing the Mekong River and heading into the green foliaged mountains of northern Laos was exhilarating. After being too young to serve during World War II, missing the Korean War by only a few years, and then having seen no combat in the Marine Corps, I was finally on my way to war.

Long Tieng sat in a narrow valley ringed by steep, rugged karsts about 120 miles northeast of Vientiane. The airstrip was dirt. Thatched huts and storage buildings formed a "U" around the northwest end of the strip. Chickens and pigs roamed freely. All of the men and boys wore green fatigues, often several sizes too large for them, and they all carried M1 rifles or carbines that seemed greatly oversized for their short frames. The Meo women wore the traditional black, full-length dress and often herded half-naked children. The density of the population in that narrow valley was significant.

The first days were hectic. I got settled into a cot in one of the rice "godowns" that I shared with Air America pilots who were over-nighting at Long Tieng. I learned that the mosquito netting over the cot was not as much to keep out mosquitoes, but to deflect the rats that fell or jumped out of the thatched roof searching for loose rice.

General Vang Pao was very congenial and seemed to enjoy practicing his English on me. He insisted that Tony Poe and I join him and an entire entourage at dinner each night at his main house. I was introduced to "Lao-Lao," the local white lightening, rice wine, sipped through long reeds from a communal pot, and a locally produced beer. After several initial disastrous forays into Meo drinking events, I learned to fake the amount I was imbibing. My gut and brain were forever grateful. Eating at Long Tieng was also an adventure, but between Vang Pao's dinners, canned goods the pilots would bring from Thailand, and the inevitable sticky rice, I survived fairly well. At harvest time we had the corn the Meos planted which, after boiling, we dipped in the cans of lard USAID provided. In my later assignment in Sayaboury Province, it was a different matter. When we were going out on a patrol for several days the village women cooked sticky rice. You took a large chunk, mashed it flat, wrapped it in large leaves and put it into your pack. You then added whatever vegetables you could eat raw. That was your breakfast, lunch, and dinner for the duration of the patrol. The Thais would get canned curries and other Thai specialties dropped to them. After a few disastrous attempts to join them in their repast, I learned that when you see a Thai shedding tears while eating his curry, that stuff is really hot!

While attempting to adjust to the constant air traffic in and out of Long Tieng, the often-chaotic military strategy discussions between Vang Pao and his commanders and Tony Poe, the rudimentary living conditions were the least of my problems. I was challenged to figure out what my role was in the middle of this seeming chaos. I knew that I could not attempt to fill the boots of Vint. I had to create my own boots. Vint had often taken a nation-building approach with Vang Pao. He had worked diligently to get Vang Pao to act not only as a military commander but also as a civic leader of his people, concerned as much about their economic well being as their physical safety in the middle of a war. At 26, I had no training or experience in that area. I had my Marine Corps tactical infantry training and the CIA paramilitary training. I decided to revert to what I knew and try to learn from actual experience as quickly as possible.

Initially, Tony assigned me to coordinate the dawn-to-dark air operations that supported Vang Pao's headquarters and field elements scattered throughout his region. This meant working with the Thai and Meo air ops coordinators to insure that the Air America and Bird and Son fixed-wing Stol aircraft and H-34 helicopters were loaded with the right ammunition, rice, and passengers. I was also ensuring that the pilots were properly briefed on their mission, the sites for either a drop or landing, and on the latest intelligence on enemy locations and activity in the area where they were headed.

In a small dusty area, a dozen fixed-wing aircraft and helicopters were constantly jockeying for position to be fueled, loaded, and pilots briefed. Meo soldiers humped 80-pound bags of rice and cases of ammo between the aircraft at the direction of the coordinators. Accidents were frequent. During my first week, a loader walked into a turning propeller, and was cut in half.

In another incident, a Pilatus Porter aircraft was loaded with eight bags in its small drop door. A Meo radio operator was being flown in the aircraft back to his village after training. The pilot was briefed that the airstrip was muddy and he should drop the rice, then land and deliver the radio operator. Dropping the rice first would lighten the aircraft's weight and make landing on the strip possible. Over the site, the pilot looked back and motioned the radio operator to the back of the aircraft, away from the trap door. Apparently the radio operator decided, instead, to help offload the rice bags through the drop door. When the pilot made his run at 800 feet and dropped his load, he pulled up and looked in the back of the plane. It was empty. The team on the ground reported to Long Tieng that night by coded message: "Aircraft dropped eight bags of rice and one radio operator. One bag of rice and one radio operator broken."

At that time, the airstrip at Long Tieng was limited to landing the STOL aircraft, the largest being the twin engine "Caribou." It had a ramp door in the back, a decent cargo capacity, and carried a pilot and co-pilot. Long Tieng itself was supplied by airdrops using C-46 cargo aircraft as well as C-123s. Winds, monsoon thunderstorms, and the narrow, mountain-ringed valley made for dangerous flying even for these larger aircraft, not to mention enemy gunfire. On a cloudy day, a C-123 came over the strip. The pilot dove, then climbed steeply as the loadmasters (kickers) in the rear of the plane released the heavy pallets loaded with ammunition that rode tracks out the back of the aircraft. One kicker was in the forward part of the aircraft, the other in the rear on the tailgate. Because of the low cloud cover, the pilot nosed the plane over immediately upon feeling the release of the cargo in order to stay below the clouds. Everything in the plane was momentarily weightless. The kicker in the front of the aircraft was not tied in. He rose in the air and the aircraft flew away from around him. The kicker in the rear reached desperately for his partner as he floated out of the aircraft past him, etching deep scratches in the second kicker's arm as he tried, but failed, to grab him. I looked up to watch the last pallet clear the aircraft and the parachutes open. I suddenly saw a human figure emerge from the back of the aircraft flailing in the air some 800 feet above me. Some of the kickers, including this one, were known to parachute out of the aircraft at the end of a run. This time there was no parachute. I watched as the body fell towards the ground and heard his scream. He hit about 100 feet away, bounced and then flattened. When I reached him, blood seeped from every pore. I'm sure his crew had nightmares as bad as mine that night.

Chapter 9

During the spring of 1964, the North Vietnamese began intensifying their military efforts along with the Lao Communist forces, the Pathet Lao. In March they attacked and captured the Plaine des Jarres, to the north and east of Long Tieng. Additional attacks were being carried out in the northeast province of Sam Neua, along the border of North Vietnam. North Vietnamese supply trucks came out of North Vietnam, along Route 7 to Khang Khay and Ban Ban.

At this time I began to fly out of Long Tieng to better learn the country and our area of operations. The Meo positions were often not much more than a series of trenches and thatched-roofed bunkers scratched out of a narrow ridgeline. In some locations there was a small village housing the families of the local soldiers. Dirt strips or helicopter landing pads had been carved out of the trees in some of the most unlikely locations. There were airstrips along the tops of ridges, in box canyons, and some that launched the aircraft into space off the end of a ridge. One of those strips was at Padong, on the south side of the Plaine des Jars. Padong had been the site of many fierce battles between the Meo and the Pathet Lao and the village had changed hands on several occasions. One of my early trips there was to assess the feasibility of flying out a long barreled Russian artillery piece that the North Vietnamese and Pathet Lao had somehow managed to haul into the site. The Meo had recovered the piece and a good amount of ammunition during their latest victory there. Vang Pao badly wanted it safe in a location closer to him.

The take-off strip was long enough in theory, with its Norwegian ski jump shape, to allow a twin-engine Caribou to land and take off. Whether the Caribou could successfully take off while carrying a heavy artillery piece that barely fit inside the plane remained to be seen. I met with the two pilots and their kicker. We went over the weight of the piece as we could best translate it from the Russian manuals. Once they decided that the weight factor might be within their capability, we had to see if we could get it into the aircraft and secure it, so it would not come loose during the trip down the bumpy airstrip or during in-flight turbulence, or upon a rough landing.

With many Meo soldiers pulling, pushing and grunting, we managed to get the gun into the plane and secured to the satisfaction of the crew. The pilot advised that we would wait until first light when the air would be the coolest and he could achieve maximum lift. He then turned to me and said that there was one additional condition to his making the attempt the next day. As the representative of those who had ordered the piece be carried out, I was to fly with him. I spent some time that night pouring over the Russian manual attempting to confirm that we had figured the weight accurately.

The next morning was clear and cool at the 5,000 foot elevation of Pha Dong. The engines cranked up. The kicker and I strapped ourselves in on either side of the gun. The Meos lined the runway to watch the foolish Americans try to kill themselves. The pilot taxied to the farthest point of the runway, turned and revved the engines to full power while standing on the brakes. I could feel the aircraft straining. The brakes were released and we rolled and jolted downhill along the runway, then started up the "ramp" at the far end of the strip. I looked at the kicker who rolled his eyes and mouthed. "Oh shit!" Suddenly we were launched off the ridge into space, some 500 feet above the valley. Did we have enough lift and airspeed to keep from dropping like a rock? For a moment it didn't seem so, but the propellers bit into the cool air, the pilot nosed down to pick up airspeed and we were flying. I said a prayer of gratitude to the Canadians who had designed and built this great plane.

Not all of my trips with the Air America pilots turned out that well. Shortly after the Pha Dong episode, I flew one of the H-34 helicopter runs from Long Tieng to a Meo-held site between the Plaine Des Jarres and Sam Neua in the northwest. Our objective was to deliver ammunition, evacuate a wounded soldier and one other, and for me to debrief the Thai Paru officer in charge. The site was a narrow ridge that had a deep ravine separating it from an equally narrow ridge held by the Pathet Lao just a few hundred yards away at the same elevation. The pilot Bill and his wife lived in the same dusty compound as Irene in Udorn. His crew chief was one of the many Filipino crew chiefs who did such a great job keeping the choppers flying. As we neared the site, I dropped down from the co-pilot's seat into the belly of the chopper below. I took the helmet and headset from the crew chief and took his seat next to the door so that I could guide Bill in and avoid the enemy fire from the opposite ridge. I kept my M1 rifle ready to return any ground fire we might receive. We made a safe landing on the lee side of the ridge, just below the ridgeline. As I jumped to the ground the Meo soldiers began to hurriedly empty the aircraft of its load of ammunition and carry the wounded man to the craft. The Thai Paru noncom and I held a brief meeting, pouring over the map. He gave me a quick situation report and I passed on instructions to him. All of this was accomplished by screaming at each other over the noise of the chopper and the small arms fire whistling just over us from the enemy held ridgeline opposite.

Mission accomplished, I jumped back into the aircraft, keyed the mike and repeated my warning to Bill to fly directly west from the position and not to the north or east. In a cloud of dust we took off, banked and turned north and east. We immediately passed the end of the ridge and into the sights of the enemy position. The takeoff had been a dangerous one and I never knew what caused Bill to turn into the enemy position. We were hit immediately. I saw a cable that ran the length of the aircraft above me splinter and several holes appeared in the chopper. I heard the engine scream as though out of control. We began spinning and I heard Bill's voice through my headset screaming: "Mayday, Mayday, we are hit and going in out of site..." At this point Bill had put the chopper into auto-rotation. The walls of the ravine flashed by the door. Bill called Udorn or Vientiane control again yelling, "Tell my wife and kids goodbye. We are going to die!" I keyed the mike and said: "Shut up and fly Bill and let dying be a surprise!" This had its intended effect as I felt the nose pull up and Bill made a remarkable three-point landing at the bottom of the ravine.

Once the rotors stopped, my first problem was to figure which side of the ridge was the friendly one and which was the enemy one. Heavy fire was coming from both of them. Seeing the muzzle flashes from one side, I figured that was the enemy firing down at us and the Meos were directing their fire across at the Pathet Lao to provide us cover. Between the unwounded soldier, the crew chief, and Bill and myself, we helped the wounded soldier up the ridge. There were enough coulars in the face of the ridge to provide us cover from the gunfire. The Paru noncom and several Meo soldiers who had said goodbye to us at their position just a short time before, soon joined us from above. Several hours later a second helicopter arrived and ferried us out. I didn't have to warn that pilot which way to depart; Bill did that.

I returned to the village of Hong Non to spend several days with Colonel Thong, a Royal Lao Army officer assigned to General Vang Pao, and the Paru corporal assigned to that location. According to our intelligence, Hong Non was to become a target of the North Vietnamese in the not-too-distant future. We laid plans for harassment tactics along the enemy supply lines and ambushes designed to forestall what we saw as an eventuality. Both Colonel Thong and the the Paru corporal had proven their considerable skills and courage in battle.

Colonel Thong died later, shot while in an American helicopter attempting to rescue a downed American fighter pilot just inside the North Vietnamese border. The Thai corporal died in January 1965 when the North Vietnamese finally attacked Hong Non. Tony Poe was badly wounded during that battle and barely escaped from the North Vietnamese.

Chapter 10

I was becoming increasingly concerned that Vang Pao was directing his forces to be more engaged in holding territory and engaging in set piece battles, than in sticking to the guerilla hit and run tactics that had been successful up to that point. Perhaps his concern over dealing with the hoards of refugees created as the North Vietnamese and the Pathet Lao pressed their offensive, drove him towards that strategy. The problem was that wherever the soldiers went, so followed their families... often in droves. That meant that when the enemy attacked their positions, the soldier's first concern became the safety of their families. While an understandable reaction, it did not lend to mobility or counter attacks. When attacked, instead of countering with flanking ambushes, the soldiers conducted rearguard actions to protect their retreating families.

My now regular and lengthier forays outside of Long Tieng had made me aware of how vulnerable the North Vietnamese supply lines were as they stuck to the few roads through north Laos and river routes that were available to them. I spent many days in the Meo positions, talking to the local commanders and

Paru advisors. They took me on their patrols. Along the Plaine des Jarres road routes, we watched from our hidden positions as the North Vietnamese trucks rumbled past us, showing no concern for attack. Along the rivers, I found the enemy supply boats; small craft totally vulnerable as they floated southward. On a number of occasions I demonstrated that vulnerability to the Meo by setting up ambushes from the banks. We blasted the boats and crews out of the water, sunk the supplies and slipped back to the Meo villages.

In order to harass the road traffic, I convinced Vang Pao to create a sniper unit. The volunteers had to be single men who would not have a family following behind. We obtained new .03 Springfield rifles with scopes and camouflaged fatigues for the recruits. My partner in this was a Thai Paru non-com who was a skilled trainer, demolitions expert and marksman. I was later to help take the bodies of this corporal and his Paru partner, from an aircraft to a burial site when the two were killed in a fight against the North Vietnamese. We trained the snipers hard. Some dropped out, but we ended up with a dozen skilled men. We taught them not only the skill of marksmanship, but also how to select a position that offered entrance and fast egress and in which they could lie for hours, invisible until their target appeared. We also taught them to recognize North Vietnamese officer insignia so that they could take out individual targets.

I obtained incendiary rounds that, when fired into the exposed gas tanks of the North Vietnamese trucks, caused them to explode in a ball of fire. We had armor piercing rounds that would penetrate an engine block and disable a truck. As a graduation exercise, we took four snipers at a time along Route 7, near the east side of the Plaine des Jarres. We maneuvered them into position, then waited for a target. We assigned two snipers to take out the first truck and successive trucks with incendiary rounds, and two others to pick off the truck crews as they jumped from their vehicles. My Paru partner and I joined the clean-up snipers in taking out the vehicle crews. At the end of the exercise, we had disabled about ten vehicles and killed over 20 enemy soldiers with no casualties on our side.

I was elated, but my elation was short-lived. For unknown reasons, Vang Pao became unwilling to begin to use the snipers on a coordinated basis. Instead of the snipers being headquartered out of Long Tieng and assigned specific missions from there as I had planned, the 12 men began to disappear, allegedly back to their home units. Vang Pao declined to discuss the issue. As my Paru partner and I downed several beers together one night, he explained that it was because of politics and pride. Vang Pao could not have anything succeed that was not his idea. If what was seen as an American initiative succeeded, he would lose face. Lesson learned.

CIA Headquarters, of all places, provided the next opportunity to pursue my quest to use unconventional tactics. The Technical Division advised that they had perfected a manner of launching rockets and heavy warheads from makeshift launchers that could be carried far behind enemy lines. They offered to send two technicians to demonstrate and provide training on the systems. This time, thanks to my Paru partner's advice, I approached the situation differently. At dinner over several evenings, I mentioned the success Vang Pao had enjoyed with his captured Russian artillery piece that we had flown out of Pha Dong. I mused over whether a makeshift rocket launch system could be developed. After several nights of poking and prodding, I got Vang Pao to instruct me, in front of everyone, to see if CIA could come up with a system to launch rockets from makeshift devices from behind enemy lines, in areas where they would not expect artillery to be used. I agreed to try.

The rapid arrival of the technicians with launchers, rockets and 55mm artillery warheads was publicly attributed to the respect the CIA Headquarters had for Vang Pao and their wish to support him in any way. My Lao language capability had not gotten a whole lot better, but my Irish BS held me in good stead. The tech folks had designed six fiberglass tubes that had been fused together, side by side. A U-shaped arm swung out from them to form a support. The arm was notched to set the angle of the tubes and the notches determined the distance and trajectory of the rockets. In this case, the rockets were the type normally fired from under the wings of fighter aircraft. The second system consisted of one fiberglass tube and a support arm. The missile in this case was 4.5 inch artillery warhead. A firing mechanism had been worked into both systems.

The launcher and rockets could be carried into position in rugged terrain where the enemy would not expect such an attack. Timing pencils were used to set the time the missiles should be launched, giving the Meo a chance to slip out of the area before they went off. In case the enemy came upon the launchers before they were fired, there was a motion sensor that overrode the timer and launched the rockets if it was moved. There was a second small charge of plastic explosives that blew up the launchers once they had launched the rockets. Thus, there would be no evidence for the enemy to figure out what hit them.

We had a very successful test of the system against a Pathet Lao position in the hills just to the west of the Plaine de Jarres. We infiltrated the area, set up the systems, set the timers and bugged out. We then watched from a distance at sunrise as the rockets ripped through the air and landed in and around the position. We never determined the number of casualties, but we learned that the Pathet Lao abandoned the position that morning fearing another "artillery attack." We continued to use the systems until the CIA Tech Unit stopped producing them, deferring to other priorities. We still had artillery rounds and some rockets left after we ran out of the launchers, so we improvised simple wooden launch racks for the rockets. We located sites in the roads used by the communist forces where the road was cut into the side of the mountain and there was a steep drop off on the outside. We dug holes at those points, planted the 4.5 artillery rounds and detonated the rounds, blowing that part of the road off the side of the mountain. This forced the North Vietnamese to dig that portion of the road further into the mountain, which they eventually did, but it was a good harassment and delaying technique that made life tougher for the enemy.

From pilots who were flying to the area east of Long Tieng, we learned that enemy crews had been busy making the old Route 4, that ran south from the Plaine des Jarres, passable for truck traffic. We began to receive reports that trucks were already heading south along the route. This meant that the enemy forces could have a route of access to the Mekong River, and then into the capital, Vientiane. I had been urging Vang Pao to send guerilla teams into the area to harass and hopefully stop the traffic, but no action had been taken.

Late one afternoon, a Porter pilot named Lloyd, who flew for Bird & Son, landed and reported that a convoy of enemy trucks was moving south on the road in broad daylight just a short flying distance away. Things were quiet that afternoon at Long Tieng and I was bored and frustrated by the idea the enemy was moving unimpeded so close to us. I don't recall whose idea it was, but we gathered a number of football-sized rocks and loaded them in the Porter. I jumped in and Lloyd flew us out of Long Tieng heading east. In a few minutes we spotted the convoy in the open. I stacked the rocks in a pile in the recessed drop door and Lloyd put the plane into a dive, coming at the convoy from the rear. Lloyd pulled the drop door release over the center of the column and down rained the rocks on the trucks. We watched as the trucks came to a halt and the crews and troops bailed out. Some of the truck cabs had canvas tops, so we had obviously done some harm. We flew home feeling a bit satisfied.

Over the next weeks, Lloyd would make it a point to pass over Route 4 on his way back into Long Tieng. If our activity at that time permitted and there were trucks on the road, we'd load up and make a "rock run." Lloyd was a bright former Alaska bush pilot who always had an idea of how to do something better. During his days off in Udorn, he got a metal shop to weld together 12 inch tubes in a frame that fit into the recessed drop door of his Porter with a lip around the frame that kept the frame from falling out when the drop door opened. The tubes, probably about 30 of them, were large enough to stack hand grenades three deep in them, one atop the other.

Lloyd arrived at Long Tieng and proudly showed me his creation. The next time he spotted trucks on Route 4, we loaded the contraption in the Porter along with a few cases of fragmentation grenades. On the way I pulled the pins on the grenades and slid them into the tubes three deep, with the handles still intact, and the bottom grenades resting against the drop door. The only bad moment came when we hit some turbulence and I had to throw my body across the tube contraption to keep the grenades from bouncing out of the tubes into the cabin. We had been varying our approach to the trucks and this time we came at them from the front. I was concentrating on keeping the grenades in the tubes, so I did not look up, but Lloyd yelled that troops were bailing out of the trucks down the hillside, so he angled over so we came directly above them. He released the door and dozens of grenades dropped earthward. Unfortunately we had an "air-burst" as the grenades apparently had short fuses and exploded not far under the plane. We had a lot of shrapnel marks on the belly of the plane for which Lloyd later had to come up with a story when he went to Vientiane for maintenance.

We didn't hang around to determine what damage we had done but headed home a bit shaken, realizing we were lucky we hadn't brought our own plane down. Back at Long Tieng we decided that in the future we would tape the grenade handles down with masking tape so the spoons would not be released until they struck the ground, soldier, or truck. In the next weeks we made several runs, experimenting with the amount of tape necessary to hold the spoon, but allow its release upon striking the ground. Although our efforts to wreak a bit of havoc on the enemy were very rudimentary, we must have been having some effect as we found out one afternoon some weeks later.

We located a convoy on the side of the mountain where there was a steep drop off and ravine along its flank. We made our grenade run and turned, then Lloyd flew parallel to the trucks at the same elevation as they were on the road. I had opened the side window and stuck out the barrel of a .30 caliber machine-gun. I was just about to open fire when I saw the side canvas flap of a truck thrown back and realized I was looking down the barrel of a .50 caliber machine gun mounted in the truck. One accurate hit from those rounds would knock us out of the sky. As the gunner opened fire and I saw black puffs of smoke, I yelled, "Dive, dive! Fifty caliber incoming!" and opened fire at the same time. Lloyd immediately nosed over, swooping to the bottom of the ravine just below the line of trucks. I continued to pour fire towards the gun, which suddenly began to fire erratically and away from us. I could only figure that my fire had caused the gunner to duck. All of this took place in the space of seconds and we had been only about 50 yards from the gun when the firing began. It was a quiet ride back to Long Tieng.

Chapter 11

The military situation in the western Plaines des Jarres in late spring 1964 was deteriorating quickly. By mid-May, traveling to Sam Neua Province and the northern Plaines des Jarres became an exercise in dodging new enemy positions as the Pathet Lao and North Vietnamese troops took control of the length of the valley and the adjoining mountains. Phou Nong, the strategic hill position south of the PDJ, had exchanged hands several times, but in the communist's spring offensive, thousands of Meos streamed out of Phou Nong as enemy fire rained down on them. The attack created an enormous refugee problem for the already beleaguered Pop Buell and his Agency for International Development staff, headquartered across the ridge to the north from Long Tieng. Pop and Drs. Jigg and Pat Weldon worked days on end with little or no rest to bring food and medical assistance to the frightened and now homeless refugees.

The enemy situation reports of the Meo and Paru units located in outposts around the Plaines des Jarres were coming fast and furious reporting the increased enemy action and the large number of North Vietnamese troops coming into the area.

These reports were collated and analyzed by the Paru Intelligence Team in Long Tieng and passed to the unit in Nong Khai for further analysis and distribution. I was traveling almost daily to various outposts attempting to confirm the reports of increasing engagements and North Vietnamese troop presence. In questioning villagers as to whether the enemy troops that had come through their village were Pathet Lao or North Vietnamese, I learned I could not always trust the observations of the villagers to distinguish between the two cadres. I quickly learned that if there were no longer any of the skinny Lao dogs in the village, then the troops had been North Vietnamese. They, unlike the Lao, thought the dogs a tasty supplement to their rice rations.

I would also press the Meo soldiers to authenticate the reports they had sent in regarding how many enemy they had killed in a particular engagement. I had been on enough patrols with them to realize that they did not usually stick around long enough after an engagement to accurately count enemy casualties. Tony Poe had his own method of dealing with the issue. Under Tony's rules, an enemy killed had to be confirmed by sending Tony the ears of the deceased enemy soldier. Tony would send a reward to the reporting unit. He kept the ears in a large hollow bamboo pipe behind our kitchen hut at Long Tieng. Reportedly, prior to my assignment to Long Tieng, the CIA management in Vientiane challenged a report of a large number of enemy killed in a particular battle. In response, the story goes, Tony sent a large manila envelope filled with a goodly number of ears to the station chief. It is said that the chief's secretary was never the same again after dipping her hand into the envelope when it arrived at her desk.

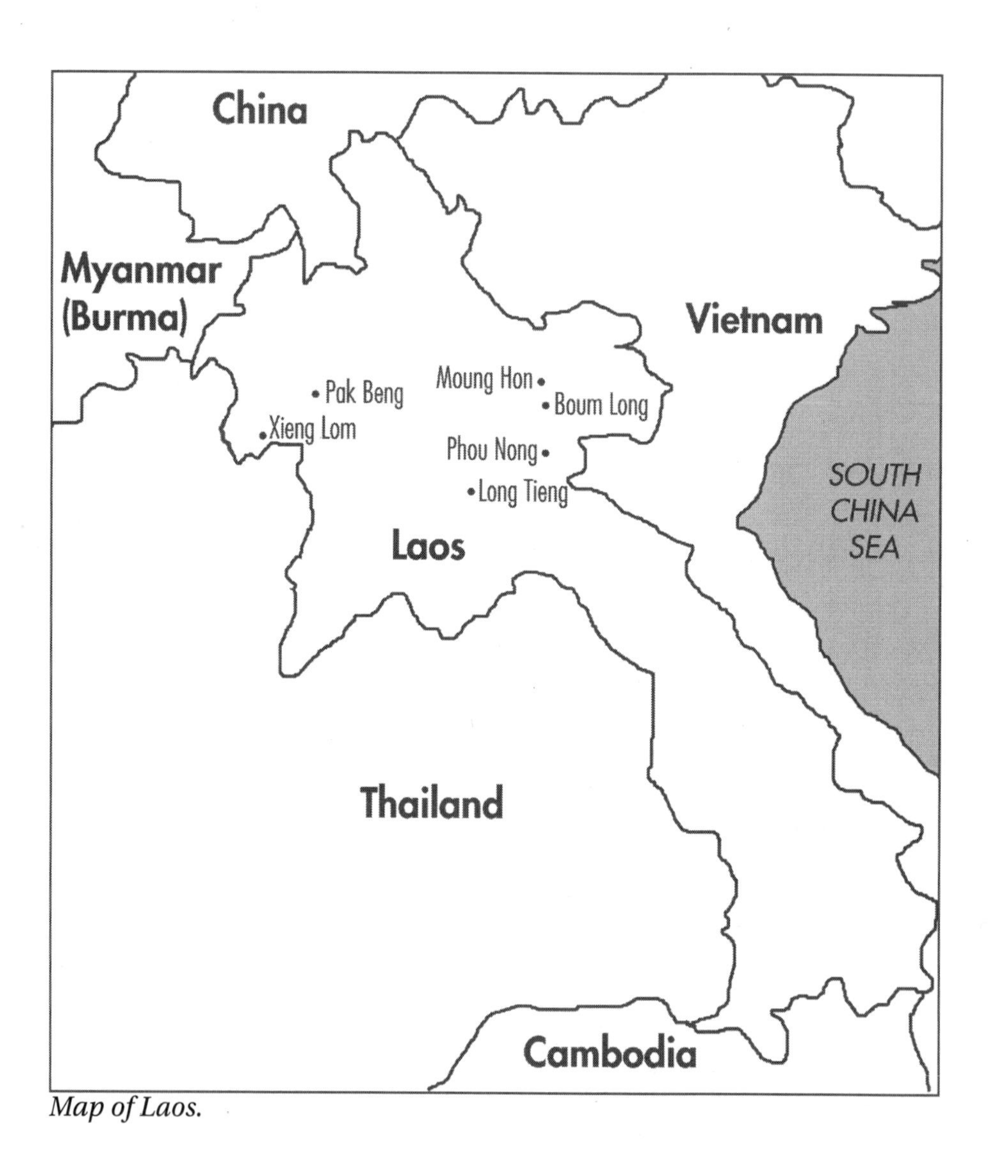
China
Myanmar
(Burma)
Vietnam
Pak Beng
Moung Hon
Boum Long
Xieng Lom
Phou Nong
Long Tieng
SOUTH
CHINA
SEA
Laos
Thailand
Cambodia

Map of Laos.

Air Ops Jack at Long Tieng.

Author in Afghanistan, 1974.

Author at Phou Nong.

Author's hooch at Sayaboury.

CIA Intelligence Star. Author and Director Admiral Raborn.

Author and Lao Colonel at Xieng Lom.

Paru Corporal and Colonel Thong at Hong Non.

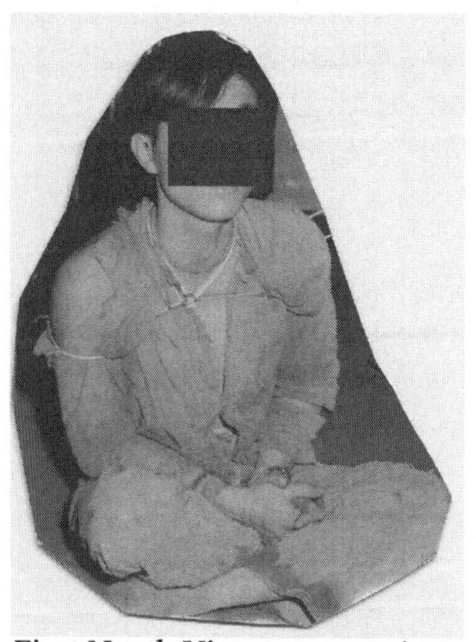

First North Vietnamese prisoner.

Improvised rockets.

Hong Non before attack.

General Ouane Rattikhone and author.

General Vang Pao and author.

Lonely outpost.

Juk's Team Xieng Lom.

Sayaboury twins.

Air resupply at forward site.

Porter crash at Long Thieng.

Alpine Rescue Team. Author on right.

Author during Alpine Rescue Team search mission.

Chapter 12

While numbers may have been exaggerated, there was no doubt that the enemy was on the move westward in increasing numbers. This reporting apparently alarmed Washington enough that the Navy was ordered to begin conducting aerial reconnaissance flights from aircraft carriers off of Vietnam over the Plaine des Jarres. Unfortunately, we were never made aware of these flights. Therefore, on June 6, 1964, when we received initial word of an American aircraft down over the Phou Nong area, neither the Air America pilot I was flying with north of the Plaines or other pilots in the area had any idea we were about to engage in a search and rescue operation for a downed US Navy Lieutenant named Charles Klusmann.

According to his account in "The Foundation," the publication of the Naval Museum Foundation, Klusmann was flying an RF-8A Crusader, unarmed reconnaissance aircraft off the USS Kitty Hawk. On his first mission over the Plaine des Jarres, he and his wingman came under heavy anti-aircraft fire. Klusmann's wing was shot up and on fire and he was lucky to make it back to the ship. On June 6, Klusmann flew what was scheduled to be his last mission. He and his wingman refueled in flight, found the Mekong River in lousy weather, and headed north on a compass heading until they broke partially clear of clouds along Route 7 towards their target of Ban Ban, on the western end of the Plaines. Passing Khang Khay, Klusmann took several anti-aircraft hits in the wing. While pulling up, there was a solid hit in the fuselage and he started losing his precious hydraulic oil fast. With his control system frozen up, he said, "Adios" to his wingman and punched out. His wingman described him making a perfect exit, going through the ejection phases until he was gliding earthward on the main parachute.

Klusmann describes gunfire being directed at him, then bouncing off the top of a tree, crashing through the branches and landing off balance with one leg out to the side. His right hip, knee and foot were badly wrenched. His wingman remained overhead until he was forced to head back to the ship before he ran out of fuel. Klusmann half crawled and half walked up the hill a ways. The gunfire stopped, it became quiet, and he realized he was in deep trouble. Eyewitnesses often have conflicting views and memories immediately after a traumatic event. After forty years the differences can become very pronounced. I have read and heard a number of accounts of the attempted rescue of Lt. Klusmann, but the best I can do is relate the attempt as I recall it. It should be explained that the principal mission of the Air America crews in Laos was to safely transport people, goods, ammunition and rice, from one location to another in support of the clandestine war. Conducting search and rescue missions in unarmed aircraft was a requirement forced upon them on an ad hoc basis when one of their own aircraft went down for whatever reason. On June 6, 1964, there was no command structure per se for such missions. The pilots and CIA and Paru personnel on scene did what they could at the moment with whatever resources they had available.

I was at Long Tieng that day when one of the pilots reported that there was a plane down just south of the PDJ. I couldn't find Tony Poe, so I jumped in a Helio Courier and headed for Site 88, on the north side of the Plaine. During the short ride there, we heard a lot of confused radio traffic regarding just what aircraft was down and where it was. Eventually we learned that it was a US military aircraft, but even this was a bit confused as the pilots and Vientiane Air America Control were being careful of what they said on open airways. It also came as a considerable shock to us that there even was US military aircraft in Northern Laos.

At Site 88 we were joined by two H-34 helicopters flown by Bill Cook and Tom Moher. We learned from radio traffic that there were three fixed wing aircraft over the Phou Nong area; a C-123, a Haviland Caribou, and a Helio Courier. They had spotted Klusmann's signal mirror and were urging that helicopters be dispatched to the scene immediately. This sounded like a great idea, however it meant that Cook and Mohr's choppers, which were the only available ones, would have to cross from Site 88 across the PDJ between Khang Khay and Ban Ban where

I knew the North Vietnamese had heavy ant-aircraft sites. One of these had just brought Klusmann down. While the urgency of the situation was well understood, both helicopters had to be refueled. We had been told to standby for mission clearance from Vientiane or Udorn and that took time to receive as well. I briefed both pilots on the best route.

I was going to ride in one of the choppers, but we decided that a Thai Paru captain would ride with Mohr and the Helio pilot and I would lead the helicopters in on the Helio. The Paru captain had been in charge at Phou Nong when it fell and knew the immediate area intimately. My maps with the enemy positions were back at Long Tieng, but I felt I could rely on my memory to steer us around the sites. If we took fire, the Helio was faster and had better maneuverability which would give the trailing helicopters a better chance.

The flight was almost surreal; three unarmed aircraft with no fighter cover, crossing the most heavily fortified enemy positions in Laos on a now sunny day just above the treetops. As we passed over Route 7, I could see enemy trucks roaring up the road in our direction, their occupants likely anxious for another kill. The radio traffic was incessant, with Control calling for updates and the fixed wing pilots over Klusmann screaming for the helicopters to get there, "Now!" I was quickly developing an understanding of the phrase, "sitting ducks".

According to Klusmann, shortly after his wingman departed the area, he heard an aircraft overhead, a Helio Courier. He set off a smoke grenade and then signaled with his mirror. The Helio pilot responded with a wing-rock and by revving his engine. A Caribou and a C-123 then joined the Helio. The three circled above Klusmann for what he described as "a couple of hours." There was no gunfire at that time. Klusmann finally heard the sound of the helicopters. He confirmed his position with his mirror and crawled up a small hill to a clearing just below the ridge line.

The fixed-wing pilots guided us in to Klusmann's position by having the Caribou dive toward it, pulling up at tree level and dropping a smoke grenade out the rear cargo door. The area around Klusmann erupted with intense ground fire. I was later told that the Caribou took a large hit in the belly as it pulled out of its' dive. Fearing a trap, I told the choppers to hold off and we made a fast pass just feet over Klusmann with the Helio. Klusmann appeared to be waving us off. I then told Cook to make a fast pass over Klusmann before trying to land, figuring the enemy was in the trees just above him, waiting for the helicopter to land. If the chopper did not draw fire on the pass, then I would have him land. At that moment, Moher apparently thought he was in a better position and he swooped by Klusmann. As he did, he took a rain of fire from the hillside above Klusmann where, as I suspected, the enemy had lain in wait for the choppers.

I saw Moher's helicopter suddenly nose down in a dive towards the bottom of the ravine between the two ridgelines. Moher was screaming on the radio. The Paru captain, in the co-pilot's seat, had taken a hit in the forehead and his blood and bone chips splattered over Mohr, the windshield and the cockpit. The Thai's shoulder harness was not locked and he fell forward over the control stick, pushing them into a dive. Suddenly, the Thai Paru regained consciousness, leaned back, reached up, and locked his harness. Despite a hole in his scalp and a bloody face, the captain managed to give Moher a "thumbs up." Moher regained control of the aircraft, turned north and headed for Site 88 trailing smoke.

From the amount of fire I had seen coming from the woods just above Klusmann, I knew we didn't have a chance to pick him up and said so on the air. I could now confirm that Klusmann was bravely doing his best to wave us away, knowing it was a trap. Cook, taking fire, turned and followed Moher. We loitered in the Helio for several minutes, frustrated and angry as we watched the enemy soldiers come out of the trees and take Klusmann prisoner. It was a bad scene. Everybody scared as hell, feeling horrible leaving Klusmann back there... the big bird pilots still screaming, not understanding what the choppers had gone through, and we still had to go back past Khang Khay and Ban Ban over Route 7 again, with the enemy now on full alert. Not the best ride any of us ever had.

I spoke with Cook some time later. I think he took a lot of heat and Moher some also, for not landing. On scene, I was the one who held them back initially and then told him to try only a fast flyby to see if they drew fire. My experience, what I saw, and my gut told me it was a trap. It was. If they had landed, they would never have taken off. They had proven themselves by flying across the most highly enemy defended area in Laos in low and slow unarmed H34s. They did not need to apologize to anyone.

Chapter 13

The rest of June 1964 saw the Pathet Lao and North Vietnamese forces continue their dry season offensive, constantly probing west and north from the Plaine des Jarres. We were under strong pressure to come up with a North Vietnamese military prisoner so that the US Government could show living proof to the United Nations and the world that the North Vietnamese had not lived up to the so called, "Geneva Accords," a formal declaration signed in Geneva on July 23, 1962, that created a coalition government and required that all foreign troops be withdrawn from the country. While the US pulled out its corps of over six hundred military advisors, the Vietnamese did not. Of course, the North Vietnamese were just as anxious to capture first Vint and/or Tony Poe, and eventually myself and/or Tony for the same propaganda purposes. There was no cover story for the two of us and being able to demonstrate that the CIA had advisors in the country would have been a coup for the Vietnamese.

With all the trips I was doing in areas that were turning over to the enemy, sometimes within hours of my being there, and fresh off the Klusmann rescue attempt that could have turned disastrous for any of us on it, I decided to create my own cover in case I was captured. On my next infrequent trip to Udorn to see Irene and the kids and to brief Pat and Bill, I rummaged through my old personal stuff and came up with my Marine dog tags. I wore them upcountry from thereon, making sure that no visiting CIA chief saw them. I had decided that, if captured, I was Terrence M. Burke, Sergeant, United States Marine Corps, serial number 1537923. I believed it would be better to be kept alive and paraded around as proof that there were still U.S. military in Laos than to be shot as a spy. I'd leave it to the US Government to sort out how they would respond to that one. I also retrieved a miniature compass that was smaller round than a dime. This I concealed, sewed into the collar tab of the fatigue shirt I generally wore.

We got the first break in our effort to capture a North Vietnamese prisoner when a Meo guerrilla unit ambushed an enemy patrol west of the Plaine des Jarres. In an unusual move, they took several prisoners, one of whom turned out, from his papers, language and uniform, to be a low ranking North Vietnamese soldier. The unlucky lad was brought to Long Tieng and placed in the Meo version of a holding cell. This was a 15 x 15 x 15 hole in the ground. The top was crisscrossed with sturdy bamboo poles, over which flattened 55 gallon aviation gas drums were laid. There was a hole cut in the center and over that a 2.5' x 2.5' rice pallet was placed as a trapdoor. A guard usually sat on the trapdoor. This precaution was virtually unnecessary, as the only way out was via a bamboo ladder that was removed from the hole and usually lay on top of the flattened drums.

Word spread quickly of the capture. I had the guards bring him out of the hole as I wanted to check his health and attempt to properly identify him. I finally found someone who claimed to speak some Vietnamese. The three of us sat on the ground, the prisoner with his hands tied behind him. The soldier was just a kid of about 17 years of age, and scared silly. I was struggling to communicate through an interpreter whose capability was considerably below that which he claimed. The ring of observers around us was suddenly broken from behind me as a roaring madman whom I immediately identified as a drunken Tony Poe, bowled me over and set himself on the prisoner with his large, strong hands locked on the soldier's throat. "Fucking Vietnamese! I'll kill you bastard!" It was very clear that Tony meant to carry out his words and in doing so, undo months of effort. By this point, the two were rolling on the dusty ground. I jumped on Tony's back and applied and arm bar choke hold on his throat from behind.

Under normal circumstances, Tony could have picked me up and thrown me halfway to Vientiane. At this point, however, he was so drunk that he as much passed out as he succumbed to my hold. He gave up on his grip of the soldier and rolled to one side. The stoic crowd of Meo just stood and watched without comment as I picked the North Vietnamese soldier and myself up out of the dust. Tony got up, muttered a few more invectives and stumbled off. I can only imagine what the Meo were thinking about these crazy Americans. I don't recall our getting very much information of any worth out of the soldier. He was so low ranking and such a pitiful sight that the powers to be in the embassy in Vientiane decided he would be of little value. He was paraded around Long Tieng for awhile, and then disappeared as so many prisoners seemed to do.

Either we had broken the Vietnamese prisoner jinx or the North Vietnamese were putting more of their soldiers in harms way, as we captured several more enemy soldiers over the next few weeks. All were low ranking, however, and aside from some personal documents and diaries, yielded little of intelligence value. They also refused to talk, except one. It was alleged that two enemy soldiers were captured together and placed in a hut for interrogation. When they would not cooperate, the interrogators supposedly wrapped primacord, a thick, explosive cord that is used to detonate larger charges from a distance, around the neck of one of the soldiers. The primacord was lit. When it exploded, it severed the head from the torso and the head landed in front of the second soldier. It was said that the second soldier talked so much over the next days that they eventually shot him to shut him up. It was not a gentle war.

Chapter 14

In early July 1964, we had yet another call to action for our ad-hoc rescue group. Mike Marshall, a helicopter pilot, was missing. Mike was a friendly, well-liked Texan who had managed to become the subject of a number of humorous stories, most of which involved his navigational skills, or lack there-of. One story had him flying across Laos and North Vietnam and mistaking the Gulf of Tonkin for a "large Lao lake," before his crew chief corrected him and he turned around, arriving back in Laos on gas fumes only. Another story had a pilot on the ground observing the wheels of Mike's helicopter sticking out of the bottom of a cloudbank into the clear blue sky while Mike was reporting he was flying on instruments in bad weather.

This time, Mike was carrying Meo soldiers and his crew chief in enemy-held territory northeast of the Plaines. They ran into bad weather in the afternoon, and Mike, thinking he was in safe territory, elected to land on a small ridge that ran parallel with a valley. The weather did not break and Mike decided they had to spend the night on the ridge, sleeping in the helicopter. According to his debriefing, Mike attempted to start the helicopter engine the next morning before daybreak, but it would not kick over. After transferring fuel from the rear tank to the front, Mike's attempt to start worked, but just as the engine coughed to life, heavy gunfire shattered the windshield and hit the aircraft. Mike cut the engine, dove out the right side, hanging upside down for moments as his foot caught under the seat. Mike pulled himself back into the cockpit, released his leg and jumped from the helicopter. He momentarily spotted his Filipino crew chief, Cristologo, who had been hit in the shoulder. Cristologo then disappeared into the brush. According to the debriefing, Mike crawled into the tall saw grass, then made his way downhill and hid in a clump of bamboo as the helicopter exploded and burned behind him. Mike heard shouting and weapons firing for several hours and then it went silent.

We had started the search at daybreak after contact had been lost with Mike the previous afternoon. I was flying in another H-34 with Sam Jordan piloting, Mondello as crew chief, and accompanied by Lao Army Colonel Thong. Sam was a rock-steady professional who began making a methodical grid search of the area where he thought Mike might be. Within a short time after commencing the pattern, Sam pointed out a charred area on the ridgeline. A close sweep revealed the tail of the helicopter intact among the ashes with Mike's tail number clearly visible. We did a quick circle of the area and spotted a nearby village that we knew to be hostile. I did a fast reckoning and figured that, if they were not already at the site, it wouldn't take the enemy in the village long to get to the burned helicopter. We were still heavy with fuel and Sam could not chance a landing on the ridge. Sam told me he would hover on the south side of the ridge where he would drop Colonel Thong and me. We would have to make our way to the top. Sam would take off, circle the area and look for any survivors nearby while he burned off more fuel. Unfortunately we had no means to communicate with Sam, and if anything went wrong we would be on our own. Colonel Thong was a fearsome warrior, though, and I figured I could not be in better company.

We ended up dropping into six-foot high saw grass that was razor-edged. The only way we could get through it and still climb the ridge was to play leapfrog. I would fall forward onto my face with my rifle stretched out in front of me, flattening the grass. Colonel Thong would step between my spread legs, then onto the pack on my back and throw himself down ahead of me. I would then stand and repeat the maneuver, launching myself off his back. It was tough going for about 20 minutes, but our adrenalin was pumping and we were sure the enemy was racing towards the site as well, anxious to bag a second helicopter.

Our initial reaction in sighting the ruins of the helicopter from the air had been to assume that it had crashed and burned. Upon reaching it, however, Colonel Thong and I could see from the position of the remains of the engine, rotor blades and other parts that the helicopter had burned in place, falling into an ashen heap. I spotted a pilot's helmet lying on its side near the wreck. I was hesitant to pick it up, fearing what remains I might find inside. It was empty, however, and not burned. I knew it meant Mike had escaped the flames. We had also spotted empty shell casings near the aircraft, so I could only assume that Mike had been shot or captured or both. At that point the enemy soldiers started firing towards the site from the path to the village.

As Colonel Thong and I looked for an escape route for ourselves, we heard Sam's chopper approaching from the valley below. Sam swooped up and over the ridgeline, hovering dangerously, a short distance from the burned aircraft. His crew chief waved frantically for us to come to the helicopter. As we ducked under the wheels that were six feet off the ground, the crew chief yelled for us to get in. I clasped my hands together, Colonel Thong immediately popped his foot into the sling I had created and as he leaped I thrust him upward and onto the floor of the chopper. I grabbed the edge of the floor and did a pull up to my chest. As my eyes cleared the edge I looked across the cabin at a tattered and bleeding Mike Marshall sprawled on the floor with a larger-than-life grin on his face. I was so shocked at the sight of him that I lost my grip and fell back to the ground. I made a second effort and, with Colonel Thong and the crew chief pulling on my pack, I joined a very happy Mike Marshall on the floor of the chopper as Sam pulled away from the ridge.

There was no time for celebration or explanations, as we were taking heavy fire from the village. Earlier I had secured a doubled cargo strap to one side of the cabin door. Now I secured it across the open door, tying it to the frame. I thrust the muzzle of a Browning Automatic Rifle (BAR) through the double strap and swung the rifle in a circle around the strap, giving me an improvised firing platform. Sam swung the chopper broadside to the village and I opened fire, picking off several soldiers who had been firing at us. Emptying two 20-round magazines in quick succession had the desired effect of silencing the enemy fire. We then got the hell out of there.

As excited as Mike was at being rescued, he immediately asked us to begin searching for his crew chief, Cristologo. Now low on fuel, however, Sam's immediate priority was to get Mike to a safe site where he could get medical attention and we could refuel. The search for Cristologo continued the next day with several additional helicopters flown by veterans such as Dick Elder and "Scratch" Kanach joining Sam Jordan and myself. Kanach was the senior pilot. At mid-day in the second day of the search we had landed in a clearing for fuel and a quick lunch. Kanach received a radio call from the Air America radio room in Vientiane. The American Ambassador had ordered that the search for Cristologo be abandoned. We all looked at each other stunned. The mainly Filipino crew chiefs were brothers to these pilots, sharing the same risks day in and day out, keeping the helicopters flying, as devoted to the mission as any man in Laos. A quiet chorus of "Bullshit!" came from the lips of all present.

Falling back on a famous phrase from World War II movies, Kanach radioed Vientiane that their message was garbled and that we could not copy. The engines roared to life, we were airborne into the search once more, and within an hour Sam Jordan had spotted a bleeding and weak Cristologo and had him safely in his chopper headed for safety.

Chapter 15

So much of what took place in Laos during this period revolved around the civilian air operations. This was primarily Air America at the time with an important role played by the smaller operation, Bird & Sons Air Service. As the North Vietnamese continued to expand their operations against the Meo, it was the ability to re-supply Vang Pao's outposts by air with everything from rice, ammunition, medicine, radios, and blankets that kept the Meo fighting. Tony Poe taught me the importance of recognizing the bravery and dedication of the American pilots and, in the case of the helicopters, their mostly Filipino crew chiefs. It was critical that the pilots had confidence and trust in us. In the rush to get multiple aircraft loaded and on their way, it would be easy to overlook giving the pilot the latest information on the conditions he could expect to encounter en route and at the destinations. Tony drilled into me the requirement to assume nothing and to give the pilot the best information you could.

To say that camaraderie with the pilots was important would be an understatement. I still count many of these remarkable men as my best friends. Not all of them were the easiest to get along with, but most of them were. They made salaries that, at the time, were amazing to someone like me who was drawing a government wage of about $5,000 a year. Yet, you rarely met a pilot who gave you the impression that he was in it for the money. With some, that may have been the original attraction, but for most, they believed in the mission and risked their lives to carry it out.

The other oft-repeated fallacy was that the pilots were knowingly and willingly carrying opium in their aircraft and financially benefiting from it. The fields of opium were a principal crop for any Meo village in an area secure enough to develop an annual crop. For decades before Air America, the Meo had developed a transport system to get the product of their crops to market. There is no doubt that they exploited the availability of the aircraft to move their opium tar. In order to understand how this occurred, however, one needs to know a typical air mission.

Whether it involved the single engine Helio-Courier, short take off and landing (STOL) fixed wing aircraft or a ponderous H-34 helicopter, most air operations had the same basic fundamentals. They landed at Long Tieng and refueled from hand-pumped 55 gallon fuel drums. Tony Poe, myself, or later, Air Ops officer Jack, would assign their load and mission, brief them on the situation and wave them goodbye. Often this was done with multiple aircraft at one time. The sites or landing strips they flew to were usually carved out of the side of a mountain with minimal length and clearance fraught with cross winds, altitude issues and, not the least, enemy ground fire. Upon landing they would usually be greeted by a hoard of milling people, anxious (to the point of walking into the propeller) to unload whatever cargo had been brought to them and to load anything and anybody they could onto the aircraft, usually just to get out the hell out of where they were. Baskets, pots, crates, pigs, chickens, you name it, would be shoved into the aircraft. In many cases, the pilots never shut down their engines, but anxiously worried about incoming enemy fire, whether the load exceeded their takeoff ability from the most marginal strip, and whether they had enough fuel to make it to the next destination.

In those circumstances, pilots did not have the luxury of inspecting each container and negotiating a price for its safe transport. Did opium get moved by these aircraft? Certainly. Was this a profit-making venture by mercenary pilots? In two years I never saw any evidence of it.

What I did see was evidence of amazing flying ability. I was constantly hitching rides on aircraft in order to visit outposts and to spend at least a few minutes with local and Thai leaders there to determine what was taking place in their areas. At night I would sit in my hooch in Long Tieng and collate and analyze the information before passing it on to Udorn. Some of these rides took unexpected turns.

On one occasion in the middle of the rainy season, I rode a twin engine Caribou aircraft that was to land at a northern strip with large bales of black cloth intended to be sewn into clothing by the Meo. When we dropped through an opening in the clouds over the village, the pilot realized that the airstrip was too muddy to safely land on. As he pulled up, he saw that the hole in the storm clouds we had descended through had closed over. We were now trapped in a bowl over the strip, closed in by mountain ridgelines we could not see. The pilot put the aircraft on its wingtip and started flying extremely tight turns over the barely visible airstrip at very low altitude. I retreated from the jump seat behind the pilots to the rear of the aircraft where I grabbed a headset and wedged myself between the bales of cloth as though they would cushion me when we hit the side of the mountain. The rear drop door of the aircraft was open and I could see flashes of mountainside as we spun our tight circle. Over the headset I heard the most remarkable, professional interplay between the pilot and copilot. It sounded like what one might hear in a movie. "Full right engine, half flaps, full right rudder, mountain dead ahead" and on and on for what seemed like hours. At one point I pulled the headset off and just prayed. At last I heard, "Sky at 11 o'clock... full power... climb you son of a bitch." Then, "OK, we're clear...how are you doing back there? That was fun, wasn't it?"

No one can minimize the effect that the local Laotian rice wine had on some of the wilder aspects of the air operations. There were always several aircrews overnighting at Long Tieng. They were always invited with the American and Thai advisors to gather at General Vang Pao's house for dinner. Most participants would sit around the huge clay jugs and take turns drinking the wine through long reeds. "Lao-Lao," the Lao's answer to Kentucky moonshine, was another mainstay. At times there was even a form of local beer available. From these sessions, operations were often hatched, many in response to our inability to strike the enemy in true current military fashion with air strikes.

Our Porter pilot, Lloyd, had long desired to improve upon our early air strikes that relied first on dropping large rocks and then hand grenades on truck convoys. From a captured North Vietnamese soldier's diary, we had learned that our effort had yielded results. The soldier had been in one of the trucks we attacked. He described the damage that had been done to some of the trucks and the soldier's fear as the grenades dropped around them and the subsequent raking of the column with machine gun fire. According to the diary, several North Vietnamese soldiers had been wounded and killed.

Sitting next to each other with reed in hand, the wine apparently fertilized the minds of Lloyd and Tony Poe as they came up with a plan. The Meos had originally been armed with .03 Springfield bolt -action rifles supplied by the CIA. As the war progressed, we had begun to replace those rifles with the more modern M-1 rifles and M-1 carbines. Tony supplied Lloyd with some of the now stored Springfields. Lloyd took these to Udorn on his next trip where there was a growing contingent of U.S. Air Force Air Commandos. Many of these airmen were also ardent hunters and the Springfield was considered a great hunting rifle. Over beers at the Air America bar, Lloyd negotiated to swap rifles for the bombs used as armament on the Air Commando's fleet of T-28 propeller driven fighters. Lloyd soon began stocking the small bombs at Long Tieng.

When it was convenient, Lloyd and Tony would have a work crew wrestle a couple of the bombs into the Pilatus Porter and the two of them would take off in search of targets. Spotting an enemy emplacement, Tony would wrestle the bomb into the drop door, arm it and Lloyd would let it loose over the target. Their debriefings and claims of success usually took place that evening over yet another jug of rice wine.

The operation did not last long, however. Technology soon caught up with them. A communications intercept operation run out of Udorn targeting radio traffic between North Vietnamese units in Laos and Hanoi soon began to pick up "chatter" referring to a noisy civilian aircraft dropping bombs on them. Curious US Embassy officials in Vientiane arranged for some overflights in an attempt to confirm the reports. Luckily we learned of the activity and the bombing runs immediately ceased. At this point, only one 200-pound white phosphorous bomb remained at Long Tieng. Having no way to safely dispose of it, it remained hidden under a stack of rice bags in one of the warehouses.

In early September 1964, the Royal Lao Air Force began to provide some long awaited tactical support by conducting raids in their T-28 aircraft on enemy positions north of Vientiane in the ridgelines near Ta Vieng. Pilot Lloyd had been dropping rice in the same area and spotted the enemy position in a mountain karst that the T-28's had been unsuccessful in locating. He exchanged radio traffic with Vientiane air control, which welcomed his suggestion that he point out the target to the fighters after he re-fueled at Long Tieng. Lloyd reported the request to me and requested a supply of smoke grenades that he could use to mark the target. Unable to locate any, I suggested that we substitute the 200 pound white phosphorous bomb for the smoke grenades. After all, it provided the desired white plume of smoke when it hit and we would also get rid of the last of the incriminating evidence at Long Tieng.

We loaded the bomb in the aircraft drop door, rigged the arming mechanism so that Lloyd could activate it himself and off he went. Lloyd rendezvoused with the fighters and made a perfect drop of the bomb on the enemy position high along the craggy ridgeline. The fighters then made their runs on the targets, but considering the probable effect of Lloyd's strike, it was overkill. Also in the overkill category was the subsequent investigation as to who had requested Lloyd to divert from his rice dropping chores to mark a tactical target for the Laotian Air Force. Documentation of the inquiry revealed the high interest of the US Air Attaché's Office, the CIA Station Chief, and Bird & Son and Air America officials. Two of the officials and an Air Force Officer took the heat for the diversion. Almost as a sidelight, a representative of the Air Attaché's Office, who had observed the target marking and Lao air strike, commented on and questioned the extraordinarily large explosion and smoke from the marking of the position. Fortunately those conducting the inquiry accepted the explanation that we had bundled a "large number" of smoke flares together.

Chapter 16

Three months had now passed since the unsuccessful rescue attempt of Navy Lt. Charles Klusmann. Despite our best efforts, we developed little information other than that he had been taken to the heavily fortified Pathet Lao and North Vietnamese Headquarters area near Khang Khay on the Plaine des Jars.

We did not know that Lt. Klusmann had fought off serious illness, solitary confinement, and the efforts of his captors to use him for their propaganda purposes. With resolute courage he had developed a plan to escape from his compound prison with several Laotian prisoners. He escaped in early September 1964. At least one of his fellow escapees was recaptured, and he and his remaining colleague, Boun Mi, were separated from the other escapees. According to Klusmann's account in the Naval Aviation Museum Foundation's publication "Foundation," Klusmann and Boun Mi evaded enemy soldiers but endured several days of crossing one steep ridgeline after another and being attacked by leeches before reaching the Meo-controlled village of Boum Long.

I was in Long Tieng late that afternoon when one of the Thai Paru officers rushed up to me holding a just-received message from the unit at Boum Long that an "American pilot" had walked into their position. I immediately realized that it could only be Klusmann. There were no other missing pilots we knew of who would have been in that area. There were missing Air America pilots who had been shot down in the Tchepone area, but that was far to the south.

I quickly took stock of what resources we had to respond to Boum Long. I knew by the time we got there it would be getting dark and most of the pilots would not want to attempt an after dark take off and most could not reach Udorn without landing somewhere in Laos for refueling; an impossibility as there were no airstrips equipped for night landings. At the same time, I could only guess that Klusmann might be in serious physical condition that would require immediate attention and I had to assume that enemy forces might be pursuing him at that moment. Boum Long was only lightly defended and an enemy force intent on recapturing Klusmann could easily overwhelm the Meo.

Fortunately, the intrepid and fearless Lloyd had just landed at Long Tieng with his Pilatlus Porter. He did some fast calculating and advised that he could take two passengers from Long Tieng, pick up the pilot at Boum Long and "probably" make it to Udorn. Lloyd immediately began topping off his fuel tanks.

Luckily, Jiggs Weldon, an American doctor who worked with the Meo for the US Agency for International Development (AID), was also at Long Tieng. I quickly briefed him, and he immediately agreed to accompany me to Boum Long. While he ran to get the medical supplies he might need, I ran to our operations shack, grabbed my M-1 rifle, and extra bandoleers of ammunition. I instructed the Paru officer to send a terse message to Udorn regarding what we had been advised, the action we were taking, and to notify General Vang Pao. Tony was not at Long Tieng, so I would have to wing this one on my own. As I started to rush out of the shack, I passed the kerosene refrigerator some of the pilots had recently provided us with. I pulled it open, grabbed three bottles of San Miguel beer, and dropped them into my light pack along with the bandoleers. The three of us were airborne in minutes. The anxiety level was extremely high during the approximate hour flight to Boum Long.

The airstrip at Boum Long was carved out of the ridge top and the village lay below to the south. Not knowing what to expect, I grabbed my weapon and ammunition and told Doc Weldon and Lloyd that I would go down to the village to check out the situation.

As I half ran down the path, I saw a group of the Meo heading for me surrounding a Westerner dressed in a muddy shirt and short trousers. He had a dark beard and a most un-military head of hair. I stopped just above him and called out, “Lieutenant Charles Klusmann?” His face literally exploded in huge grin and smile and he looked up and saw me and shouted, “Yes, yes!” Tears filled his eyes as he ran to meet me with a hug. Klusmann later told "Man's World Magazine," that hearing an American's voice call out his name was one of the greatest moments of his life.

We were quickly joined by Doc Weldon, who immediately began to assess Klusmann's physical condition. I spoke to the local Meo commander, whom I knew. He said that Klusmann's fellow escapee, Boun Mi, had approached one of their outposts alone, then after convincing the soldiers of his identity, had waved to Klusmann to join them. The commander gave me the few details Klusmann had provided him on his escape. I asked if the commander thought the enemy might be in pursuit and the commander said he had already assumed that would be the case and had established his meager defenses accordingly. We agreed we should get Klusmann out of there immediately and not wait for morning.

Speed was not that easy to achieve, however, as when I explained that we could take out only one passenger due to takeoff weight limitations, Klusmann immediately resisted. He was not about to leave Boun Mi behind. It took a lot of convincing that the commander would look after Boun Mi and that we would get him out the next day for Klusmann to relent. Then there were pictures for Doc Weldon to take of Klusmann and Boun Mi. Finally we were in the aircraft and a very nervous Lloyd headed the aircraft down the marginal runway as dark settled on to the top of the mountain. Lloyd swung the plane south and into the black night sky. Nobody flew at night in Laos. The Porter had a single engine. One malfunction and that would be it. We were too buoyed by Klusmann's happiness to dwell on that possibility though.

Once underway, I had Lloyd radio Vientiane and Udorn Control that we had made a successful pickup and that the "cargo" was in good condition. We then settled back on the floor of the plane. I suddenly remembered what I had put in my pack. At that moment Klusmann was repeating, "I can't believe it, I can't believe it!" I pulled out a bottle of still cool San Miguel beer from my pack, popped it and handed it to him. His eyes opened wide, and he said, "Now I know I'm dreaming." During the rest of the trip to Udorn, Doc Weldon attended to Klusmann's multiple cuts and leech bites. Klusmann and I exchanged details of what had happened from our respective positions the day of his capture. I was relieved when he confirmed that he had waved off the helicopters knowing that the enemy soldiers were just above him waiting and using him as bait.

As we approached Udorn, Lloyd was instructed to land and taxi to a warehouse location some distance from the main hangers and Air America offices. We did so and observed a blue sedan with Air Force markings. Next to it stood two uniformed Air Force Officers. Not sure of what we were supposed to do, Lloyd kept the engine running and I jumped out and ran to the officers to obtain instructions. After being upcountry for several months I apparently looked pretty unkempt to the officers who grabbed me and shouted: "You made it Lieutenant, you made it!" Over the noise of the plane's engine I had to explain that I actually "didn't exist" and that Klusmann was still in the aircraft. We got Klusmann out of the plane and into the car. Lloyd, Doc Weldon and I headed for the Air America bar. I didn't see Klusmann again until many years later when he and his wife visited us in our home in Colorado.

Chapter 17

In the fall of 1964, Vint returned from his lengthy medical leave. By this time there had been many changes at Long Tieng. The enemy offensive had pushed westward. Many of the larger Meo villages had fallen and refugees were pouring into Long Tieng and to Site 20 to the north. The former villagers of Long Tieng were now spread across the valley and into the mountain karsts. The use by the North Vietnamese of the route from North Vietnam through Laos and then into South Vietnam was now openly acknowledged by all political elements and named "The Ho Chi Minh Trail." With the increasing support of the CIA, the Meo and General Vang Pao had become a political force in Laos, a fact not welcomed by all the Lao politicians in Vientiane. The number of CIA personnel working inside Laos had increased.

Vint quickly resumed his role as chief advisor and political advisor to Vang Pao. While Tony Poe's drinking during Vint's lengthy absence had blunted his effectiveness, he had still managed to keep Vang Pao on track and to keep him from taking the North Vietnamese and Pathet Lao forces head on as Vang Pao was sometimes inclined to do. I strongly supported this strategy and continued to recommend and plan guerilla-style forays against the enemy's supply and communications lines. The military situation had changed dramatically in Vint's absence, and not in our favor. The North Vietnamese were obviously on the move. It was clear that Vint's concentration on building the economy and political stature of the Meo and Vang Pao, and my concentration on guerilla tactics for their survival, didn't necessarily mesh.

In Udorn, Bill and Pat apparently recognized that it was time for me to move on. Bill, for some time, had been considering a retreat route for Vang Pao and his people. As it became increasingly apparent that the Meo might not be able to withstand the pressure of the ever-growing and more aggressive Vietnamese forces, Bill decided to reactivate his earlier plan to establish a retreat location in Sayaboury Province. Sayaboury was located in the southwest portion of Laos, adjacent to the Thai border and south of the Mekong River. The mountains were not as severe as in the north, but its rugged valleys could support the farming talents of the Meo. Should conditions really turn bad, the Meo could slip across the porous border into Northwest Thailand. There were already Meos living in the province along with Lao Theung and other Laotian hill tribes. There had been no reports of North Vietnamese troops in Sayaboury to that date. Pathet Lao forces continued to raid Meo villages and control some villages previously controlled by the Meo and Lao Theung, but they were not a highly organized or sophisticated force.

Bill and Pat decided to send me to Sayaboury to work with the Meo to eliminate the Pathet Lao presence there. While no one mentioned retreat, I sensed that I would be establishing an infrastructure to support Vang Pao in a worse-case situation. A major change in Lao operations was the fact that I would not be working with a Thai Police Paru Team, but with a team of Thai paramilitary specialists. This decision was the result of political maneuvering within the Thai Government. Fortunately for me, the leader of the Thai Team, code name Juk, turned out to be a capable and enthusiastic leader.

My arrival at Sayaboury was without fanfare. There was no airstrip at our new location yet, and initially we had to negotiate the terms of our presence. I landed by helicopter a few miles away on a ridge line and met up for the first time with my four-man team. They had already secured a small hut in the Meo outpost for themselves. For several weeks, while we negotiated with the local leaders, I slept in a long, dirt floored hut with an extended family of local Meo. It was winter and the nights were cold, so there was always a fire smoldering in the middle of the hut. Because there was no chimney or hole in the thatched ceiling, there was always a fog of smoke enveloping us. A bamboo framework ran the length of one side of the hut. More bamboo had been split and secured to the frame to make what passed as a bed.

I had a very thin, CIA-developed sleeping blanket, and I was shown my place on the twenty foot by five foot bunk. My Meo housemates used old rice bags and scraps of cloth for their blankets. Bed time was when the sun went down. My limited Meo language ability resulted in very short fireside chats. Once the dozen or so of us settled in, the challenge of sleeping began. There were a number of aggressive snorers in the group. Then there was the old man, two bodies down, puffing on his opium pipe. I'll never forget that fragrance. Two bodies to the other side was a young couple locked in a seemingly endless attempt to extend the family lineage. Because I was a six-footer in a five foot space with no room to curl up, I developed some very sore ankles as they hung over the bamboo frame.

Our first task was to turn a small mountain village into a training location for the Meo. This included hacking an airstrip out of the jungle, building huts to live in, and fortifying our position for the enemy attack we assumed was inevitable. Once these tasks were completed we turned to recruiting, outfitting, and arming the Meo. I concentrated on learning the area and developing intelligence on the location and activity of the Pathet Lao. Two facts became clear early on: the Pathet Lao in the area were a pretty pathetic and poorly led force, which turned out to be fortuitous as the Meo we trained did not have the drive and military acumen of their brothers to the north. The days were long and the nights longer.

The Thai Team had done the best job they could recruiting about 100 Meo and Lao Theung tribesmen from the nearby areas.

The CIA had perfected the outfitting requirement by creating a 100-man "package" of fatigue hats, shirts, pants, and sneakers all packed in strong cardboard boxes that could be air dropped to locations such as ours, where the remote air strip could only accommodate the smallest aircraft.

My request for an air drop of a 100-man package was approved. This was to be followed by a drop of weapons (M-1 rifles and carbines) and ammunition. The day of the drop was met with great excitement by the Meo. Most were looking forward to their first pair of shoes. The orange cloth signal panels were placed on the dirt strip. The Thai Team scurried from group to group, warning them not to try to catch the boxes as they floated to the ground. We had seen too many locals do this in the past, only to be crushed by the heavy boxes or pallets of arms or ammo.

We heard the approaching C-46 aircraft but, unfortunately, they did not respond to the contact I attempted via my emergency ground-to-air radio. We watched in confusion as the aircraft flew over and beyond us, heading southwest in the direction of the Thai Border. A few miles past us, we saw the plane's nose tilt skyward and the load of boxes with trailing parachutes emerge from the rear of the plane. It suddenly dawned on me that, by mistake, they were dropping to a village where remnants of Chinese Nationalist leader Chiang Kai Shek's Kuomintang Army (KMT) lived. These troops had fled Burma in the late 1950s, some returning to Nationalist China, but some taking refuge in southern Laos and northern Thailand where they carried on the opium trade they had started in Burma. Now they were apparently being treated to new uniforms and shoes.

The KMT's intelligence network knew of our presence a short distance from them, as we knew of theirs. However, not knowing where their political sympathies lay, Captain Juk and I were hesitant to just drop in on them and demand the return of our goods. We therefore dispatched the our village leader and his deputy on foot to the KMT village to negotiate the return of the "package." They returned that evening and advised that the KMT leader was quite friendly and agreed to return the uniforms as long as we would allow them to keep the sneakers. This seemed a reasonable trade-off as the KMT probably did not want to be seen parading around in U.S. military fatigues by the Pathet Lao or others. The next morning we sent back an affirmative response and notified them we would transport the uniforms via our Meo soldiers on foot and by a few helicopter loads.

I had already requested a helicopter for support and within a couple of days of the drop, Air America pilot Jack Conner showed up with a new pilot he was checking out. We loaded a few spare bags of rice and headed for the KMT village with our village leader. We landed without incident and were introduced to the KMT leader. They could well have used the new uniforms as they wore mainly local civilian garb with only remnants of their former KMT uniforms. The KMT leader welcomed the gift of rice and showed us around his village. It was an extremely poor place and the soldiers I saw were not an impressive lot. During my visit Jack shuttled the boxes of uniforms that were left from those carried away the preceding day by our Meo. After noting as much as I could regarding the weapons and supplies of the KMT, I returned to our village and reported my observations to Udorn via the Thai Team radio operator, who tapped the coded message out on his radio key. I also requested replacements sneakers for the very disappointed Meo recruits.

Winning the population of the area over was one of our challenges. One of our Thai Team members had undergone the U.S. Special Forces paramedic program and was doing his best to treat as many of the locals as possible. This effort was hobbled by the local Meo "witch doctor." The Meos were animists. I came to understand that meant they believed in spirits that inhabited natural objects. In practical terms, it meant that if a child was very ill, the witch doctor would require the parents to buy (often from him) an animal/chicken, whatever, that he would slaughter and anoint the child with the animal's blood. The doctor would forbid the parents to bring the child to our medic until the child's condition was such that death was a certainty. By that time, being too late, the child would die and the witch doctor could say the Thai medic had killed it.

Realizing that I couldn't reverse centuries of tradition, I took the practical way out. I put the witch doctor on my payroll. The health of the community began to improve rapidly thereafter.

The fact that the mountain people longed for and appreciated medical assistance was brought home to me by two Lao Theung tribal women. One morning there was a noise at my hut door. I came out to find two of these shoeless, diminutive ladies standing there with a small basket containing a few eggs and vegetables which they offered me. In my very basic Lao I asked the reason for the gifts. They explained that the one lady's husband had brought their sick baby to us. Our Thai medic had treated the child and provided the needed medicine. The child was taken home by the father and was there doing fine. The ladies were here to say thank you with their basket.

When I asked where they were from, knowing that ours was a Meo village where they would not live, they pointed west across two ridge lines. They had walked, barefoot, for three days to say thank you and were now turning to head back to their village. It was one of the most moving experiences of my time in Laos. I gathered whatever cloths, utensils and food that I could give them for their trip back. It was a humbling moment, watching them walk west into the sunset.

There were light moments occasionally. During the Meo New Year one of the village elders came to me with his two daughters dressed in their best holiday finery. My Meo vocabulary was still pretty basic, but I understood he was asking me to "take" his two daughters. As I struggled to make him understand I was honored by his request, but was already married, Juk happened by and listening to the conversation, quickly burst into laughter. He finally explained to me that the man was trying to get me to take his daughters photograph. Greatly embarrassed, I grabbed my camera from my hut and took the photos.

During this same period I had been frustrated over the lack of air support to move rice and ammunition to the outposts I had established. I sent continuous messages to Tony Poe at Long Tieng asking for the use of an aircraft. Finally the Meo New Year's festivities lowered the activity at Long Tieng enough for Tony to spare me an aircraft for the day. The pilot arrived with a big smile and a note from Tony. The note was terse, "When are you going to start killing somebody over there?" Attached to the note was stapled a pair of dried ears from Tony's collection. During the day I pondered my response to Tony. Inspiration came that afternoon when I paid for a large water buffalo to be slaughtered for the village's New Years feast. I had the water buffalo's male appendages cut off, and placed in a plastic bag attached to my note. Later that day when the pilot returned to Long Tieng he delivered the hefty male organs and note to Tony. Tony roared as he read the note: "We're fighting REAL men over here".

Actual combat was sporadic and very low level. We led patrols towards Pathet Lao held villages, only to have the PL flee when our patrols were spotted. Despite the training of the Thais, the ambushes we set up were often ineffective because the Meo began firing before the enemy entered the killing zone. On one occasion the village leader took a Meo patrol to raid a nearby Pathet Lao village. A runner returned to our site and reported that the leader's 14-year-old son had been shot and wounded and was lying on the side of a hill above the village exposed to enemy fire. His father and the rest of the patrol had retreated to the ridgeline above him, afraid to rescue him. I grabbed my M1 and, with a couple of members of the Thai Team, took off for the village.

Upon reaching the patrol on the ridge I saw the boy laying below me, crying out for help. I had the Thais give me some covering fire and maneuvered down the hill and took up a covered position just above the boy. There were only two or three enemy soldiers firing from behind a log barrier they had erected at the entrance to the village. There was an opening in the logs and the soldiers moved into it, fired, and moved back. While I couldn't see them, each time they moved into position they blocked the sun behind them. I took aim at the opening and fired the next time it went black. The sun immediately reappeared and there was no return fire. The opening went black a second time, and I fired a second time. Again the sun shown and there was no return fire. I saw the third and remaining soldier from behind the logs running in the opposite direction out through the village. I decided to let him go and not shoot him so that he could tell his friends how bad we were.

We recovered the boy, and the Thai medic treated his leg wound. We went down to the now deserted village and found two bodies behind the barrier. They were shabbily dressed in partial uniforms and their weapons were dirty. Shortly thereafter the Meos reoccupied their old village.

We had gone through a number of engine failures with the H34 helicopter, but I encountered my first with the single-engine Helio Courier fixed wing, while flying from Laos to Udorn, Thailand in the spring of 1965. The pilot was new, having just arrived in country after flying for the U.S. Forest Service in Montana. We were at about 5,000 feet when the engine started coughing and the manifold pressure began dropping. The pilot was not able to correct the situation and so advised Udorn Control. He also told them he thought he had enough power to make it to Udorn.

While not a pilot, I had logged many hours in the Helio and had taken "lessons" from a number of the pilots. My thought had always been that if the pilot was ever hit by enemy ground fire I'd be well served to be able to get out of the area and attempt a landing. I had followed the same strategy with the H34 helicopter. Under good conditions I had made take-offs and landings and on one occasion flew on instruments through a thunderstorm on the same route for several hours before succumbing to vertigo. I pointed out to the pilot that we were losing 500 feet of altitude every few minutes and were not going to make it the 150 miles to Udorn at that rate and that we had better look for a place to put the aircraft down.

The concept was great, but we were flying over a dense teak forest in northern Thailand and there was nothing but a closed sea of green, tall, large teak trees below us and no sign of civilization. Luckily, over my shoulder from the co-pilot's seat, I spotted a gash in the trees and pointed it out to the pilot who turned in that direction. He was new to the aircraft and obviously rattled as he also reached up between us and started twirling the crank on the ceiling that lowered the trailing flaps on the rear edge of the wings that were designed to slow the aircraft before touchdown. We were still a distance from what now appeared to be a logging trail in the forest and too high to activate the flaps as it only reduced our forward progress. I reached up and reversed the crank, drawing the flaps back into the wing. "Not yet", I told him.

As we approached the logging trail we observed that there was only a short stretch that was not under trees and in the middle of that area a tall teak tree had been downed. It was hung up in other trees and stretched across the trail about 15 feet in the air. There was no time or power to go over it. As we headed straight for it, the only thing I could do was to cross my arms in front of my face and hope that the tubular frame cage of the aircraft would absorb some of the impact. Although the pilot did not have much time flying this model aircraft, he was an experienced pilot. He had obviously collected himself as he suddenly dipped the nose down and then up before the front gear hit the ground and we skidded under the fallen tree, coming to a stop just beyond it. I uncovered my face and we looked at each while simultaneously uttering, "Oh shit!" in disbelief.

Udorn Control had dispatched a helicopter which arrived a while later and found just enough room to land on the logging trail and take us out. The helicopter crew stopped long enough to look with amazement at what must have been one of the great

Helio landings on record. We all wished we had a camera with us to record the event. I believe that later they had to dismantle the aircraft and lift it out by helicopter.

After several months of organizing and training to the extent we could, the decision was made to move our operation north about ten miles to Xieng Lom, which was located in a wide, north - south valley where there was an old airstrip. We were instructed to build a large, wooden, operational headquarters and a large warehouse. Lumber was brought in, and the construction was soon underway. There wasn't much for me to do during the construction so I concentrated on conditioning by doing wind sprints up and down the airstrip and following an old Charles Atlas training routine from a book an air crew had dropped to me at our earlier site. I usually ran in my bare feet to toughen my soles. I had learned that the North Vietnamese took a Western prisoner's boots from him as the soft soles of Westerners didn't get them far in the jungle and mountains.

This also provided an opportunity for the Thai Team to take some much needed R & R to Thailand. During the absence of our medic, there were two incidents that challenged the very basic emergency medical knowledge that had been part of the paramilitary training. The first occurred when a villager arrived after carrying his teenage son the ten miles to Xieng Lom on his back. They had been cutting trees as part of the annual slash and burn system to clear land for planting. Not only did the smoky haze cover the country making flying even more dangerous, but many injuries occurred. Somehow, this boy's leg had been severed at the thigh. Someone had wrapped a tourniquet around the upper thigh and a cloth around the stump. The boy was still conscious and not complaining. I gave him a styrette of morphine, washed the leg with saline solution and rebound it. Fortunately I was able to get an aircraft in the same day and have him evacuated to the Tom Dooley hospital in Moung Sing.

The second case came shortly after. One of the local soldiers had apparently sold an anti-personnel mine to an older villager. The mine was a plastic explosive contained in a plastic casing about the size of a can of tuna. A horseshoe-shaped ring served as a safety. The idea was to put the mine in a shallow hole, pull the safety, cover the mine with leaves, and wait for someone to step on it. Although the mine was U.S. made, I had never seen them supplied to or used by any of our Meo troops. In any event, the villager planned to take the mine to a stream, place it in the bottom after pulling the safety, and then throw rocks at it from the bank. The idea was that the concussion and blast would kill nearby fish. The problem was he had pulled the safety, then tripped as he walked down the bank of the stream, and instinctively squeezed the mine so as not to drop it. The resulting explosion had torn off his right arm just above the elbow, ripped a flap in his chest and another gash that opened his scalp from eyebrows to hairline.

Villagers carried him to our headquarters and laid him on the bamboo table that served as our eating place. They rushed in to locate our medic, only to find me. I grabbed the medic's supplies and my CIA medical manual and headed to him. I'd put some battle dressing on the wounded before, but this wiry man was a real mess. After giving him a couple of styrettes of morphine, my first concern was the bleeding stump of his arm. I pulled the flaps of skin together and rolled them upwards to the protruding bone. Then I took some large stitches to hold the skin in place. After a couple of battle dressings and a lot of gauze wrapping, the blood was now oozing, not pouring. We had no blood for transfusions and I probably would not have known how to effect the transfusion in any case. For the chest and forehead flaps, I opened my CIA manual to the section on stitches and tried to follow the instructions, given a working area much more delicate than the arm.

The results were not pretty, but the flaps were somewhat in place. I poured more saline solution over everything and took a deep breath. Only then did I realize that a large crowd of villagers and soldiers had gathered around our open-thatched eating hut. Their stares were divided between the bloody patient and the now bloody "medic," who had not even had latex gloves.

Next, the patient needed to be carried inside our quarters, and a message requesting a helicopter for a critical evacuation had to be sent. The only communication, however, was by an encrypted radio message that an operator tapped out in code while a helper on the reversed bicycle-like hand generator provided power for the radio. This took place in late afternoon, so I knew there would be no chance of a helicopter until the next day.

That night I sat on the floor next to the patient. Between slumbering off from time to time, I gave additional shots of morphine, changed the dressings on the arm, and wiped the reduced blood seeping from the chest and head flaps. This continued through the next morning and early afternoon. Finally, in mid afternoon, I heard the "whack-whack" of the helicopter blades, followed by the dust storm as the Air America aircraft settled on to the runway. As we prepared to carry the patient to the aircraft, the pilot climbed down, arranged for re-fueling and approached us. He turned pale at the sight of the patient; however, the patient himself was in reasonable spirits and had never moaned or complained during the entire process. I'm sure the morphine helped, but these were what we would call today "tough dudes."

A month or so later, I was getting ready to settle in for the night when there was a tapping on the open door frame. There stood my wiry old patient, a stump of an arm and the ugliest forehead scar you have ever seen. He was grinning ear to ear and opened his shirt to show an equally ugly scar on his chest. He said he had been taken to the Tom Dooley hospital where they had cut off more arm bone and sewn him up properly. He said he had been asked by the doctors who the hell had sewn him up. I took that to mean they were probably not being complimentary.

My patient was alive, though, and appreciative. To show his gratitude he had brought a bottle of "Lao-Lao", the previously described local "white lightening". There was no choice other than to celebrate his homecoming with him, for which I suffered dearly the next morning.

Pilot Jack Conner and his trainee pilot returned to Xieng Lom to fly supply missions to our outlying posts for me. When they took a break at noon they were amazed to see that the locals had captured a fat tree lizard that measured some five feet in length. The pilots stayed overnight with us, and because they had kindly brought a case of beer to share with all, everyone was in a mellow mood. When our soup dinner was served, Jack was effusive in his compliments to the cook. After completing most of the broth and the large chunks of white meat, Jack asked what had become of the lizard. As the table quickly silenced, Jack looked down at the large chunk of meat in his bowl, turned white, and exclaimed, "Oh no!"

Always looking for a variety of food, several days later I walked to the west side of the village and along a path into a fairly open area. I had seen a number of tall, almost crane-like birds fly into that area. I carried my CIA provided .22 caliber survival rifle, all parts of which could fit into the stock, making it very compact and floatable. Suddenly I saw a large, maybe four-foot-long snake heading down the path directly in front of me. More from instinct than anything else, I raised the rifle and fired. The sight of flesh jumping from the snake's back was confirmation that I had hit it. The snake then left the path and disappeared into the low grass.

Realizing I had left the village vulnerable to an angry, wounded snake, I left the trail and proceeded in the same direction taken by the snake. After a short distance I found that the snake had gone into a hole, but only partially as at least a foot of his tail was still above ground. As I had done in the Marine Corps at Camp Pendleton when we hunted rattlesnakes to sell their meat and venom, I grabbed the snake's tail intending to pull it clear of the hole, throw it into an open area, and then finish it off. It didn't budge. As I pulled harder, a movement to my right caught my eye. There was the other, lethal end of a king cobra coming out of a second hole, striking at my right leg. His cape was fully extended, and it was doing its best to sink his fangs into my leg. My hold on its tail kept it from quite reaching me. It was clearly one of those, "What do I do next?" moments. I put the muzzle of the semi-automatic rifle literally into his mouth and fire several rounds that blew off the back of its head.

I waited for the body to relax and then pulled it from the hole. I had parachute cord in the "escape" pack I always carried on my web belt with a canteen of water. I slipped a loop around the snake's head and tied it to a length of sturdy bamboo. Although dead, reflex action caused the snake to partially curl around the pole. I dragged this back into the village. A few villagers came forward to see what the "farang" (foreigner) was up to now. Suddenly the cries of "jong ang" reverberated throughout the village as the occupants fled into the jungle.

After convincing them that the cobra was dead, the villagers returned and proceeded to skin it. I didn't have bird that night, but that roasted snake was not all that bad. After this, my local name became "Jong Ang." While the locals and Thais claimed it meant king cobra, I wondered if really meant "crazy American."

I occasionally had visitors at Xieng Lom. The first was the only member of Congress whom I ever saw in Laos. I will have to say he arrived without a staff and with only one U.S. Embassy representative. It was obvious that he had done his homework and was very familiar with what we were doing. The big concern he expressed was the fact that the few CIA personnel in Laos were vulnerable to capture and that our "combat" appearance would be exploited by the enemy's propaganda. I was actually in Levis and a khaki shirt at the time, but I wore my escape belt and pistol as always. The congressman suggested that I should try to pass myself off in dress as a U.S. Aid and Development (USAID) officer, doing community development work.

In the midst of this conversation, a helicopter landed. Out from the door jumped Mike L, who had just been pulled out of an almost overrun village after fighting off an enemy attack for three days. A weary Mike approached us covered with dust, dressed in fatigues, with bandoleers hanging around his neck, hand grenades clipped to his belt, and a carbine in his hand. "Who the hell is that?" asked the congressman. "That's our local USAID rep," I replied.

The most unwelcome guest was Royal Lao Army General Ouane Rathikoun. His tailored uniform could not hide the obesity that was the result of his indulgent life style. He had come to complain that by my keeping the Meo busy chasing Pathet Lao, they had little time to tend to their cash crop, opium. While my naïve picture of opium at that time was not some kid shooting up heroin in Chicago or Los Angeles but an old man sleeping next to me smoking his pipe, I still knew it meant a large source of revenue for General Ouane. The afternoon visit did not go well as I would not back down. General Ouane departed without a handshake, and I knew I had made an enemy.

Having done in Sayaboury what I had been sent there to do, on a trip to Udorn I complained to Bill and Pat that I was spinning my wheels where I was and wanted more action.

Chapter 18

My break finally came in early May 1965, but at the expense of my CIA colleague, Howard. He had been sent from Udorn to a location north of Xieng Lom, about 25 miles north of Pak Beng, a small town on the Mekong River. The site was a small village. It was not far from both the Chinese border and from Dien Bien Phu, North Vietnam. Howard started hacking out a small airstrip just north of the village and setting up a small camp for him and my Thai Team under Juk that had moved there with him. In a short time, however, Howard came down with typhoid fever and was evacuated to a hospital in Bangkok.

I received a message to leave Xieng Lom and take Howard's place, literally overnight. I received no briefings as to the mission there, but the presence there of my team under Juk and visits by my friend, the Royal Lao Army Colonel, was all I really needed. They advised that our location would be a forward operating site for combined Meo (Hmong) and Lao Theung (an ethnic minority) area defense teams. Our immediate job was to build a basic airstrip for STOL aircraft, set up a weapons and ammunition cache and to start recruiting and training local volunteers.

I didn't really like the location. The village sat in a long valley that headed north. The river, Nam Oun, ran through the village and then south to the Mekong. The mountains just to the west were under enemy control. Muang Houn, a short distance to the north, was an enemy stronghold. As was my practice, I immediately met with the village elders. I came away with the distinct impression that they had seen it all before with foreign "advisors." The French and US Special Forces had all come in promising development and peace, only to get booted out by the North Vietnamese and Pathet Lao Forces. Looking at the enemy held mountains around me and the sad-looking recruits in front of me, I couldn't help but think that our fate might parallel that of the French and U.S. Special Forces.

The next couple of weeks were spent using charges to clear and complete the short dirt airstrip, setting up defensive positions and outposts, and running fairly short patrols out of the area. Little did I know that at night a 15-year-old villager named Xieng One was slipping out of the area and reporting our activities to patrols of the 408 Pathet Lao Battalion and their North Vietnamese advisors who lurked in the nearby foothills.

Late afternoon on May 20th, I was in the midst of bathing in the shallow stream between the village and the camp when Bird & Son pilot Ernie Brace came back to my site on his last trip that evening after making air drops to outposts. Ernie came in fast and low over the trees in his single engine Pilatus Porter STOL aircraft and made a straight-in landing without circling first. I wrapped my sarong- style “pakama” around me and, as always, slipped on my pistol and shoulder holster as I walked to the plane. As usual, Ernie and the Thais kidded me for the fact that I carried my pistol even down to the stream with me while taking one of my cold-water baths. I gave Ernie a hard time about landing before we had the chance to put out the bright orange cloth strip signal indicating it was safe to land. Ernie said he would be flying to Chiang Mai, Thailand, that evening but returning in the morning. He would be stopping at Xieng Lom in the morning to bring our Thai Team radio operator to round out our team.

The Lao colonel had advised me that he had been ordered to leave our location that night and proceed to Luang Prabang. Strangely, the order had come from no less than Royal Army Commander General Ouane Rattikhone. As noted, I had crossed swords with Ouane at Xieng Lom when he learned that my training of the Meo there had interfered with their opium harvesting, a product that he had the monopoly on throughout that region. I would not back down when he met me in Xieng Lom to discuss “the problem.” In reflecting on the events that followed on May 21st, I could not help but think he had known of, or encouraged the pending attack and pulled out the Lao colonel to save a member of the Lao royal family.

In any event, Ernie agreed to drop the Colonel at Luang Prabang on his way back to Chiang Mai. Ernie asked if he could bring me anything from Thailand, and I said that a case of beer would be most welcome.

The evening of May 20th was a pretty relaxed one. We had a new Lao Army lieutenant colonel from Vientiane with us. I talked with the colonel about setting up a stronger perimeter defense and he assured me that all had been done. I shared a small hut with Juk and our Thai interpreter, Sam. Sam had gone to high school in Washington D.C. where his father had been stationed as military attaché at the Thai Embassy. He was one of the only Thais I had met who needed to shave daily. Our 15' x 15' hut consisted of a raised bamboo sleeping rack on each side of the hut that was separated by a dirt path in the middle with an open doorway at each end, one facing the river and village and the other north to the airstrip about 50 yards away.

As was my usual practice in that area, I slept that night with my trousers and boots on with all my personal gear, weapons, ammunition, and grenades laid out on the mat next to me so I could reach them quickly. About 5:00AM I was awakened by a loud noise and discovered that the bamboo wall of my hut next to me was missing. We were under heavy attack and a mortar round had taken the side off the hut. The first round was followed by a second. Most of the fire appeared to be coming from the south near the village, but there was also machine gun fire from the area of the airstrip. I yelled at Juk and Sam to get out of the hut and cover the area to the north.

The two enemy soldiers who ran in the door of my hut as I was cutting up my enemy-and-friendly-positions map didn't see me as they turned to the right and started spraying the room with machine guns. I raised my M1 and killed both of them. I looked up through the debris and smoke, and saw many more of their comrades running up from the riverbank towards the hut. I grabbed the wooden box that held some of my papers and the local payroll, put that under one arm and, with my rifle in my right hand, ran towards the front of the hut and out the door.

As I exited the hut, I tripped on the bamboo floor frame, fell, and dropped the box. I hit the ground and rolled over in the old Marine Corps manner as the place where I had just landed was punctured with bullet holes. At this point my pistol popped out of its holster. I didn't see or recover it. The gun was later seen by Ernie Brace in the possession of one of the North Vietnamese officers. My mind was racing. I could see the Lao soldiers dropping their weapons and deserting us. We were badly outmanned. I calculated whether I should save the last bullet for myself rather than risk capture and the execution that would follow for an acknowledged CIA operative. The answer "No" came quickly, as I decided I could beat them, even if captured.

I gathered the Thai team in the brush area between the huts and the airstrip, and we organized a counter attack against the huts. Suddenly, our Lao colonel turned and ran towards the huts on his own. Before we could even cover him, he was hit by a hand grenade, and lost most of his hand. He dropped with shock. I ran to him, grabbed him, and was pulling him back when I was hit by something, either a grenade or bullet fragment, that sliced into my forehead. I was bleeding but not badly wounded.

The Laos had now deserted, and I ordered the Thai team to pull back on the far side of the airstrip. As we came up the bank of the strip, a machine gun from the airstrip opened up on us. We were pinned down until I threw a couple of grenades over the berm that silenced the gun. Instead of crossing the strip, we moved east along it towards the end of the airstrip to a burned off knoll. I called out for the Lao unit that was supposed to be on top of the knoll to open up with their mortar and recoilless rifle. We soon found that they had already left for other parts, taking the recoilless rifle and mortar. In all of the confusion we were separated from three of our Thai Team members.

The enemy soldiers began to run onto the airstrip, moving up towards us in military formation, dropping and firing as they came. I was able to pick off some of them. My Thai team leader, Juk, was shot in the foot. Others took less serious wounds. I had a Lao soldier and a former Pathet Lao prisoner who was with us carry Juk back off the far side of the hill towards the trees while Sam and I held off the oncoming enemy. The wounded colonel, whose hand I had earlier wrapped with battle dressing and given a shot of morphine, was helped by two other Laos.

I heard the advancing enemy soldiers yelling orders, but I couldn't understand their Lao. They were well-out fitted with back packs, ammo belts, and helmets, which were luxury items for the Pathet Lao. I asked Sam what Lao dialect they were speaking. He said, "That's not Lao that is Vietnamese!" My reply: "Now we're really in the shit!" While receiving more return fire, the follower on my M-1 snapped, broken, out of the receiver. Of all the thousands of M1 rounds I had fired in the Marine Corps and CIA, I had never seen this failure, nor could it have occurred at a worse moment. Simultaneously, one of our Lao soldiers who had remained with us until then, frozen and refusing to fire, broke and started to run away. I reached out and grabbed him, pulling his M1 from his grasp. I also grabbed the ammo bandoleers he had around his neck. He could have cared less and just took off running when I released him. I was back in the fight.

When I saw the small party with Juk reach the cover of the jungle, I told Sam to cover me while I dropped back and took up a firing position; then he dropped back while I covered him, leap-frogging. It started to rain and we were quickly muddy and slipping up the slope. As he passed me, Sam stopped, looked at his muddy pants, ran his hand over his unshaven beard and declared, "I must look like shit!" I said, "Keep on running, or you are going to look like dead!"One of the enemy got so close to us that I bounced a hand grenade off his chest. It dropped in front of him and exploded. I was later told that we had killed seven and wounded twenty-eight.

We pulled back into the jungle and joined the others. I put Juk on my back and carried him as we moved about a quarter mile further east. I located a position for an ambush. I moved the group a hundred yards past it and had Juk, the Colonel, the ex-Pathet Lao and a couple of others hide themselves in the brush. Sam and I then moved back into the ambush site from where we could cover the route we had taken from the camp. It wasn't long before we spotted movement coming towards us. We knew that two of us could never take on the entire force, so our plan was to inflict enough damage and fear to get them to back off. We opened up with as much fire as we could muster and threw grenades as fast as we could. The enemy retreated and returned to the airstrip.

It was now several hours since the attack had begun. Sam and I remained in the ambush position. I had taken a graze round on the inside of my thigh that burned from my sweat and the rubbing of my pants, but was not serious. The forehead scratch had stopped bleeding and was crusted over. Sam just needed a shave and shower. I shared my canteen of water with Sam. It had stopped raining and the sky had cleared. We soon heard a Helio-Courier aircraft overhead. I didn't know it then, but Lou O'Jibway, a long-time CIA case officer, had been on his way to visit our site. The enemy opened up on them before they landed, and they flew away. I heard later that they had radioed in a warning that the strip was overrun. Then we heard Ernie Brace's Porter approaching the strip.

I was surprised to hear it coming closer and closer. Ernie and I had discussed the safety signal the night before, and I hoped that he had remembered my warning about it. The aircraft kept coming in from the west. This time the enemy held its fire. I could tell that Ernie had landed and had taxied to the east end nearest to me. I heard the engine rev up to full pitch as he attempted to take off again, having seen the bodies on the strip. Then I heard the enemy's weapons fire and the engine stopped. I felt really helpless at that point.

Ernie had worn a flight helmet that day, but because the Chinese air traffic communicators kept up an annoying, continuous chatter that boomed right into his ear pieces, Ernie had turned off his radio after leaving Xieng Lom with our radio operator, two Laotian soldiers, one of the soldier's wife and baby, and food supplies. His Filipino flight mechanic, Tony Alfonte, stayed back at Xieng Lom due to the heavy load. As he approached my site, Ernie switched on his radio and reported his approach to the now over-run strip. As soon as he did, he turned the radio down or off. At that moment, every controller and aircraft in the area broadcast the warning in strident tones, "Don't land, LS-174 in enemy hands!" Ernie never heard the warnings.

As Ernie's bullet-ridden plane coasted to a halt, Ernie looked back to see one Laotian soldier jump out of the plane and be shot dead. The soldier's wife was wounded. Brace and our Thai radio operator were pulled from the plane and led away towards the huts by the enemy soldiers.

I desperately wanted to go back to find out what happened, but at that point all but two of the Laos who had remained with us took off on their own, and we were left with myself, Sam, the Pathet Lao ex- prisoner, and the two wounded, both of whom we had to carry on our backs. My responsibility at that point was to the wounded. We circled further east and then started moving south.

My plan was to circle to the south and spot the river that would guide us towards Pak Beng. During a brief rest stop I lay next to one of the Laos, an older villager. He told me that I was the third foreign advisor over the years with whom he had been chased from my now-captured site. One had been a Frenchman following the battle of Dien Bien Phu and the second a U.S. Special Forces Green Beret. "You," he said, "are the first who had his boots on."

About two hours later, a Helio Courier passed overhead. I was able to signal the Helio with my mirror. We continued to move south. At about 2:00PM, we saw an Air America H-34 helicopter above us. Former Marine pilot Phil Goddard with Lou O'Jibway, who had switched aircraft, responded to my signal mirror. As they circled a small field, I set up perimeter security. They landed and the wounded were loaded aboard. I ran to the helicopter, climbed the landing gear to the co-pilots hatch where O'Jibway sat, weapon at the ready. I yelled at him over the roar of the rotors that Sam and I were going to round up more Lao soldiers and return to our now-captured site to determine Ernie's fate. O'Jibway yelled right back, telling me he was under orders to get me out of there and there would be no argument. O'Jibway was a full-blooded O'Jibway Indian from northern Michigan, nearly six feet tall and 250 pounds who had fought Joe Louis in exhibition matches during World War II. I was not about to argue with him. Reluctantly, Sam and I climbed into the belly of the helicopter, and we were flown to Xieng Lom where the rescue operation was being organized.

Upon arrival at Xieng Lom, I was told that there were USAF F-105s overhead at our now-captured site. I directed them to hit my ammunition storage area in the camp as well as some known enemy locations in the area. Air America helicopters were able to pick up the other members of our Thai team who had been separated from us early on in the firefight. One of the pilots that over-flew the captured site stated that he thought he saw a person still behind the wheel of Ernie's Porter. Based on this, we organized what we hoped would be a rescue mission.

A Thai captain had arrived at Xieng Lom to assist. The captain and I were close friends, and he was among the bravest and most battle-wise of the Paru. The Thai and I boarded an Air America H-34 helicopter piloted by Dick Casterlin and co-pilot Robbie Roberts. Casterlin was not crazy about the idea of landing on an enemy-held strip, but he was a pro and carried out the flight flawlessly. At about 5PM that afternoon we landed on the strip about 25 yards from Brace's Porter. We weren't alone, however. At our request, six of the top Air America pilots circled above the strip in Lao T-28 fighters. As the helicopter landed, three T-28s took one side of the airstrip each, spraying the borders with their 50 caliber machine guns. As planned, the Paru captain covered me while I ran to the plane. I was afraid to open the door because I figured they had booby-trapped it, so I stood up on the strut and looked in, but the plane was empty. I turned and started to run towards the huts, but there were still Vietnamese there and they opened up with heavy rifle fire. Our own T-28s also almost hit me. I had gone through a lot to get out of this place and now I was back, and I thought I was going to die there after all, thanks to friendly fire. The Thai captain and I were forced back into the chopper. Because of darkness setting in at this point, we had to return to Xieng Lom for the night.

There was heavy air activity for the next several days over that entire area. I flew with Bob Hamlin in the Beachcraft Barron and guided the T-28s led by Jim Ryan on strikes on nearby enemy positions and in dropping leaflets announcing a reward for Ernie's and our radio operator's release. During the next days and weeks while we continued the search, we tried to pinpoint Ernie's and our Thai's location so that we could launch a rescue operation. There were several Meo commando units standing by to respond as soon as we knew or had a good idea where Ernie might be. Unfortunately, our information was always late. It would only be after they were moved on to another spot that we would learn where they had been. We knew he had been taken to Mung Sai and treated very badly there and then we heard that he had been moved northeast towards Dien Bien Phu. At this point we lost all trace of them.

During the second day of the search, two H-34 helicopters piloted by Dick Elder and Ray Semora followed a T-28 flight and landed troops a mile from the site. On their second trip in, according to Elder, they picked up the Laos who were the surviving passengers on Brace's flight and our Lao radio operator. The survivors reported that at the time of the attempted rescue the night before, the T-28s had caused great confusion and they were able to make a run for it.

In bad situations there is often a lighter side. One of the escapees, our Lao radio operator, had been tied up and held outside my hut. According to him it was clear that my capture had been the objective of the raid, reinforcing my theory of General Ouane's involvement. The North Vietnamese officers had personally searched my hut. They brought out my photos of former world strong man Charles Atlas doing his very muscular exercise routines. They asked the radio operator who it was in the pictures. Tongue-in-cheek, the radio operator replied, "The American advisor." According to the radio operator, one officer looked at the other and wryly exclaimed, "I'm glad we didn't catch him."

Another light moment was when the enemy soldiers searched Ernie's aircraft and discovered a burlap bag with the case of canned beer and a block of ice. Not having seen ice before, they dragged the sack to the edge of the strip and assigned two soldiers to guard it. The hot sun took its toll on the block of ice as the day wore on. The officers almost shot the two soldiers when they returned and found the ice had disappeared.

Not so light was that Ernie and our Thai were marched north through Moung Xia and Moung Kheo, and eventually to Dien Bien Phou. After years of being caged and two unsuccessful escape attempts, Ernie was moved to Hanoi to the infamous

Hanoi Hilton prison from where he was released in March 1973, seven years after his capture. Our Thai radio operator was not released when the Americans were, but remained a prisoner for several additional years.

Chapter 19

The North Vietnames attack came shortly before the end of my Lao tour. We had been the first family in the Agency's Lao program. The family had taken the separation and living in Udorn and then Bangkok well, but it was time to move on. Irene and I went to a Thai military hospital where we visited and said good-bye to Team Leader Juk, who was recuperating from his wounds. Juk would eventually become a very senior Thai officer and then a very influential senator.

My return to CIA Headquarters was quite anti-climatic. There was a new head of the Special Operations Division, not the grizzled old paramilitary veteran who had recruited me, but a young bureaucrat, full of himself. I was advised that the new chief wished to see me. I was ushered into his office. He came out from behind his massive desk, shook hands, and motioned me to a seat in front of his desk. He retreated behind his desk into his leather chair. "Terry," he said, "I've been reading about all of your exploits, but I wanted to take the time to hear your story from you. Tell me, what was it like there in the Congo?"

After coming back from Laos, we took up residence in Virginia, in a quiet suburb. Re-entry from the jungle skirmishes of Laos, and the death I had seen and dealt, seemed unremarkable to me at first. I had been there to defeat and kill enemy soldiers, as I had been trained. But one night when I was sleeping in the Virginia house, a neighborhood kid lit some cherry bombs on the front lawn. The next thing I knew, I was out of bed in the dark, gun in hand, slowly raising the curtains and taking aim out on the street.

I was spared much of the controversy and ambivalence many soldiers experienced about the Vietnam War. Having gone to Laos in 1963 when the Vietnam War had not yet fully cranked up but was still being fought with special forces, I was spared the brunt of the political fallout. I went into Laos concentrating on paramilitary operations. We didn't read newspapers. The big picture wasn't always clear. There were air operations going on that we didn't even know about, and as we stood an extremely high risk of capture, we were informed only on a need to know basis.

When I reported back to the CIA headquarters at Langley, I had two surprises waiting for me. I received the Agency's Intelligence Star for Valor which was presented by Agency Director Admiral Raborn and Deputy Richard Helms. Only 16 medals had been given out since the Agency's inception in 1948 and the previous medal had been awarded to U-2 spy plane pilot, Gary Frances Powers, after his return from captivity in the Soviet Union. The second surprise was that Douglas Blaufarb, the CIA

Station Chief in Laos whom I had only met once in Udorn, had nominated me to be the first Agency internal candidate for the Junior Officer Trainee Program (JOT), which was later named the Career Trainee Program (CT). The Agency had always recruited young (and mostly males) from top universities and colleges, most of them with master's degrees to be JOTs. The program was a two year course in how to be a "classic" spy. It was a combination of a world economics and political course, reports writing taught by New York Times veterans, room bugging and, most important, agent development, recruitment and management. It was the best personnel evaluation, motivating, and management course one could ever hope to take.

After months of psychiatric interviews and panels, I was accepted. The training program matched the mystique that surrounded it. The two years of training were followed by eight months of training in an Asian language. Given my lack of language ability, it was an excruciating eight months. I did end up back in Southeast Asia for three years, but had only the rare chance to use the language I had labored over.

In late 1969, I was posted back to Headquarters to be an up and coming branch manager's "horse-holder"...or special assistant. Shuffling papers, no matter that it was for a very senior manager to whom I could attach myself to his coattails, was just not my career ambition though.

Whether the leaders realized it or not, 1970 ushered in the decade of the decline of the Agency. There were few opportunities for promotion, even for the most experienced intelligence operatives. The decline was later culminated by President Jimmy Carter's appointment of Stansfield Turner as Director. Turner went on to tear the Clandestine Service apart, firing the veterans who knew the art and value of human intelligence and attempting to replace them with satellites. I can't say that I saw all of this change coming, but I did know that risk takers were becoming less popular.

In the meantime, I had contacted an old Federal Bureau of Narcotics friend from Rome, who had transferred to U.S. Customs. The Federal Bureau of Narcotics had become the Bureau of Narcotics and Dangerous Drugs (BNDD) and the new agency was growing fast. My Agency experience, he said, in handling informants and working outside of the United States, would hold me in good stead.

After an interview with the BNDD Deputy Director, whom I had also known in Rome, I said my good-byes at Langley, received the blessing of the Chief of Clandestine Operations, and started life over as a federal narcotics agent.

Epilogue

My 21 year career as a federal narcotics agent, first with the BNDD and then after it merged with elements of U.S. Customs and became the Drug Enforcement Administration (DEA) in 1973, provided the opportunity to use experience I had gained at the CIA, and again work with a team of dedicated men and women towards a challenging goal.

Following an intensive training program in Washington DC, I graduated first in my class, which meant that I could choose my first office of assignment. That was easy; Miami was in the center of the Colombian and Cuban cocaine wars and the DEA office managers, supervisors and agents there were some of the best. I learned a lot from them and had some great operational opportunities. These were crammed into a short six months, however, as in the fall of 1971 President Nixon ordered BNDD to immediately double their then meager international presence. Because I was among a handful of younger agents with foreign experience, I was re-assigned to Kabul, Afghanistan. Pack bags again, pull the four kids out of their new school, again, and head for Kabul.

The two years in Afghanistan, and, for a period, covering Pakistan and India as well, were as challenging as possible. They provided a number of firsts: the first U.S. law enforcement agent to work undercover in Afghanistan, Pakistan, and India and to develop cases that could be prosecuted in the United States and in all three countries; the first U.S. law enforcement agent to be invited to Moscow to brief Soviet officials (on Afghan smuggling routes through the Soviet Union); and the first "rendition" of a U.S. fugitive, Timothy Leary, from Afghanistan to the United States. This while dodging the Afghan corruption that permeated from the royal palace down through the police. Fortunately the great support of the U.S. Embassy, from the late Ambassador Robert Neuman, his Deputy, Samuel Lewis, and members of his staff, helped to clear many obstacles. Complementing their assistance was that of one or two heroic Afghan police officers and a senior Afghan Ministry of Justice official.

At one point I tried to repay the support of Ambassador Neuman by myself and DEA Agent Michael Holm protecting the Ambassador during a planned kidnapping attempt by the "Black September" Palestine terrorist group.

Our departure from Kabul was no less complicated. My wife had left for the States a little early with three of the kids, leaving son Sean and I to complete the packing. We were interrupted by the military coup that deposed the King. Again, I was dodging around Afghan obstacles, but this time it was their tanks, roadblocks, and aerial strafing, to check out possible escape routes for embassy staff at the request of the Ambassador.

We returned to Miami, but not for long, as I was transferred to Washington DC to the internal affairs staff, which was not an assignment of my choosing. A stint followed as the executive assistant to the head of operations and then on to the Washington Field Office, supervising investigations in the greater Washington DC metropolitan area. I was then plucked out of there with only two days notice and sent to The Hague, Netherlands, to replace the head DEA agent who had been ordered out by the U.S. Ambassador. That was the start of four years in the Netherlands working with the Dutch National Police, the Amsterdam and Rotterdam narcotics squads, and superb DEA colleagues.

I returned to D.C. after the Netherlands, and took on assignments as the number two for the Denver Division and, subsequently, Agent in Charge of the Phoenix Division for the State of Arizona. In 1988, I was brought back to Washington as Deputy Chief of Operations and Intelligence. A year later I was named the deputy head of the agency. Within six months, Jack Lawn, one of the best Administrators to ever hold the office, retired and left me in charge of the agency in an acting capacity while still holding down the Deputy position. Later that year, a political appointee was named as Administrator. I carried on as his deputy for another six months, giving him time to make his own selection for that position. In March 1991, I retired after a total of 34 years of military and federal service.

After leaving government service, I went into the world of international business intelligence, investigating mergers and acquisitions, illicit trade, and conducting due diligence as an investigator in the private sector. I worked out of London often, when not from a mountaintop home in Colorado.

There were intricate and instructive cases, including an 18-month investigation for a billionaire who had been bilked out of his business by the Swiss Government. The cast of characters included paid-off Swiss lawyers and a Swiss judge, a Libyan spy in Bern, the terrorist Abu Nidal, Moammar Khadafy, and former PLO leader Yasser Arafat. It led me to a meeting with Arafat's head of intelligence in the PLO's then fortified headquarters in Tunis, with Nidal's terrorist kidnapping chief in Cyprus, and a PLO operative in Paris. The latter meeting was surveilled by both PLO and French intelligence teams. The French apparently erroneously thought I was still working for the CIA and that I was running a forbidden unilateral operation on their turf. I was forced to beat a hasty retreat to Switzerland.

Another lengthy case included investigating the players in a major post-Soviet industry dispute in Siberia that included murders in Moscow and Siberia, Russian hit men, and an attempted assassination in Israel. For a while I was running a circuit between London, Moscow, and Tel Aviv which eventually drew its own official attention.

My time in Laos and Afghanistan had taught me to value the ability to work on my own. My choice to move up the management ladder in DEA was principally based on the factor that it meant that I had to take orders from fewer people the further up the ladder I went.

With this in mind, in 2001 I left the investigative group I had been with for the past ten years and began a new phase of my career as the owner of my own company, T.M. Burke International LLC. I had developed many of the clients I worked with at the former firm and most of those chose to carry on with me in my new endeavor.

To ensure that I maintained my required level of adrenaline and need to continue to scare myself on a regular frequency, in 1994 I had joined a mountain search and rescue team, The Alpine Rescue Team, headquartered just west of Denver. Once again, I found a group of skilled and dedicated people looking to what the team described as, "Helping out someone who is having a bad day". Just the element I needed.

During the selection process for team candidates, the leaders questioned how I handled difficult situations, and I related a couple of incidents from my CIA and DEA days. Later, after completing the 12 weeks of training and final selection as a team member, I participated in my first search and rescue mission with the team. During the post mission critique, the mission leader asked me if I had enjoyed the mission. I replied that I had and found it refreshing as it had been the first search and rescue mission in my career during which I had not been shot at.

After eight years on Alpine and hundreds of missions participating in technical rescues of climbers at altitudes up to 14,000 feet, lengthy searches for lost hikers in the middle of the night, and digging out buried avalanche victims, I found that age was catching up to me. In my mid-sixties at this point, I was one of the oldest active field members. Carrying a 40 pound litter and your pack of nearly equal weight at altitude was a challenge better handled by younger members. When harassed by those young hard chargers though, I would reply, "That while I could no longer be the first one to the top of the mountain, at least I'd know what to do when I got there." A move to Southwest Colorado in 2002, sealed my resignation from the team.

The last 11 years of international business have been professionally and financially rewarding, but more importantly, have kept me mentally engaged and aware of the global events that impact our personal worlds.

My years in Laos, the courage of my colleagues there, and the strife that we suffered and inflicted as soldiers in the Secret War are never far from my mind. Like the legacy of Vietnam to so many, Laos kept part of your soul. I'm at peace with that.

About the Author

Terrence M. Burke heads T.M. Burke International LLC. which he formed in 2001 after ten years with a private investigative firm. Burke's private investigative career followed 30 years of law enforcement, intelligence and national security experience with the U.S. Marine Corps, The CIA and DEA. Burke's government service included extensive international assignments in Western and Eastern Europe, the Middle East, Asia and Latin America.

From 1960 to 1970, Burke was a CIA intelligence operations officer, primarily in Southeast Asia. In 1965, he was awarded the CIA Intelligence Star for Valor.

Burke held many foreign and domestic positions at DEA from 1970 to 1989 including Country Attache in Kabul, Afghanistan, and The Hague, Netherlands, Deputy Agent In Charge of the Denver Division, Agent in Charge of the Phoenix Division, and Chief of DEA's intelligence and enforcement operations in Washington DC.

From 1989 to 1991, Burke was Deputy Administrator of the DEA, and concurrently served as Acting Administration for six months in that period. Burke regularly testified before Congress and appeared frequently on national and international television networks. He was the agency's principal contact with the National Security Council, CIA and the Departments of Justice, Defense, State and Treasury.

From 1994 to 2002, Burke was an active field member of the Alpine Rescue Team, participating in hundreds of technical rescues and searches in the mountains of Colorado.

Burke specializes in complex litigation support cases, merger and acquisition cases, due diligence investigations, and counterfeit product investigations worldwide.